www.EffortlessMath.com

... So Much More Online!

✓ FREE Math lessons

✓ More Math learning books!

✓ Mathematics Worksheets

✓ Online Math Tutors

Need a PDF version of this book?

Please visit www.EffortlessMath.com

SSAT Middle Level Math Prep 2020-2021

The Most Comprehensive Review and Ultimate Guide to the SSAT Middle Level Math Test

By

Reza Nazari & Ava Ross

All inquiries should be addressed to:

info@effortlessMath.com

www.EffortlessMath.com

ISBN: 978-1-64612-309-4

Published by: Effortless Math Education

www.EffortlessMath.com

Visit www.EffortlessMath.com

for Online Math Practice

Description

SSAT Middle Level Math Prep 2020 – 2021, which reflects the 2020 - 2021 test guidelines, is dedicated to preparing test takers to ace the SSAT Middle Level Math Test. This comprehensive SSAT Middle Level Math Prep book with hundreds of examples, abundant sample SSAT Middle Level mathematics questions, and two full-length and realistic SSAT Middle Level Math tests is all you will ever need to fully prepare for the SSAT Middle Level Math. It will help you learn everything you need to ace the math section of the SSAT Middle Level test.

Effortless Math unique study program provides you with an in-depth focus on the math portion of the exam, helping you master the math skills that students find the most troublesome. This SSAT Middle Level Math preparation book contains most common sample questions that are most likely to appear in the mathematics section of the SSAT Middle Level.

Inside the pages of this comprehensive SSAT Middle Level Math book, students can learn basic math operations in a structured manner with a complete study program to help them understand essential math skills. It also has many exciting features, including:

- ✓ Content 100% aligned with the 2020 SSAT Middle Level test
- ✓ Written by SSAT Middle Level Math instructors and test experts
- ✓ Complete coverage of all SSAT Middle Level Math concepts and topics which you will be tested
- ✓ Over 2,500 additional SSAT Middle Level math practice questions in both multiple-choice and grid-in formats with answers grouped by topic, so you can focus on your weak areas
- ✓ Abundant Math skill building exercises to help test-takers approach different question types that might be unfamiliar to them
- ✓ Exercises on different SSAT Middle Level Math topics such as integers, percent, equations, polynomials, exponents and radicals
- ✓ 2 full-length practice tests (featuring new question types) with detailed answers

SSAT Middle Level Math Prep 2020 – 2021 is an incredibly useful resource for those who want to review all topics being covered on the SSAT Middle Level test. It efficiently and effectively reinforces learning outcomes through engaging questions and repeated practice, helping you to quickly master Math skills.

About the Author

Reza Nazari is the author of more than 100 Math learning books including:
– **Math and Critical Thinking Challenges:** For the Middle and High School Student
– **ACT Math in 30 Days**
– **ASVAB Math Workbook 2018 - 2019**
– **Effortless Math Education Workbooks**
– **and many more Mathematics books ...**

Reza is also an experienced Math instructor and a test–prep expert who has been tutoring students since 2008. Reza is the founder of Effortless Math Education, a tutoring company that has helped many students raise their standardized test scores—and attend the colleges of their dreams. Reza provides an individualized custom learning plan and the personalized attention that makes a difference in how students view math.

You can contact Reza via email at:
reza@EffortlessMath.com

Find Reza's professional profile at:
goo.gl/zoC9rJ

Contents

Chapter 1:

Fractions and Mixed Numbers

Math Topics that you'll learn in this Chapter:

- ✓ Simplifying Fractions

- ✓ Adding and Subtracting Fractions

- ✓ Multiplying and Dividing Fractions

- ✓ Adding Mixed Numbers

- ✓ Subtracting Mixed Numbers

- ✓ Multiplying Mixed Numbers

- ✓ Dividing Mixed Numbers

Simplifying Fractions

☑ A fraction contains two numbers separated by a bar in between them. The bottom number, called the denominator, is the total number of equally divided portions in one whole. The top number, called the numerator, is how many portions you have. And the bar represents the operation of division.

☑ Simplifying a fraction means reducing it to lowest terms. To simplify a fraction, evenly divide both the top and bottom of the fraction by $2, 3, 5, 7, ...$ etc.

☑ Continue until you can't go any further.

Examples:

1) Simplify $\frac{12}{30}$

Solution: To simplify $\frac{12}{30}$, find a number that both 12 and 30 are divisible by.

Both are divisible by 6. Then: $\frac{12}{30} = \frac{12 \div 6}{30 \div 6} = \frac{2}{5}$

2) Simplify $\frac{64}{80}$

Solution: To simplify $\frac{64}{80}$, find a number that both 64 and 80 are divisible by.

Both are divisible by 8 and 16. Then: $\frac{64}{80} = \frac{64 \div 8}{80 \div 8} = \frac{8}{10}$, 8 and 10 are divisible by 2,

then: $\frac{8}{10} = \frac{4}{5}$ or $\frac{64}{80} = \frac{64 \div 16}{80 \div 16} = \frac{4}{5}$

3) Simplify $\frac{20}{60}$

Solution: To simplify $\frac{20}{60}$, find a number that both 20 and 60 are divisible by. Both are divisible by 20.

Then: $\frac{20}{60} = \frac{20 \div 20}{60 \div 20} = \frac{1}{3}$

Adding and Subtracting Fractions

☑ For "like" fractions (fractions with the same denominator), add or subtract the numerators (top numbers) and write the answer over the common denominator (bottom numbers).

☑ Adding and Subtracting fractions with the same denominator:

$$\frac{a}{b} + \frac{c}{b} = \frac{a+c}{b} \qquad\qquad \frac{a}{b} - \frac{c}{b} = \frac{a-c}{b}$$

☑ Find equivalent fractions with the same denominator before you can add or subtract fractions with different denominators.

☑ Adding and Subtracting fractions with different denominators:

$$\frac{a}{b} + \frac{c}{d} = \frac{ad+bc}{bd} \qquad\qquad \frac{a}{b} - \frac{c}{d} = \frac{ad-bc}{bd}$$

Examples:

1) Find the sum. $\frac{3}{4} + \frac{1}{3} =$

Solution: These two fractions are "unlike" fractions. (they have different denominators). Use this formula: $\frac{a}{b} + \frac{c}{d} = \frac{ad+cb}{bd}$

Then: $\frac{3}{4} + \frac{1}{3} = \frac{(3)(3)+(4)(1)}{4 \times 3} = \frac{9+4}{12} = \frac{13}{12}$

2) Find the difference. $\frac{4}{5} - \frac{3}{7} =$

Solution: For "unlike" fractions, find equivalent fractions with the same denominator before you can add or subtract fractions with different denominators. Use this formula:

$\frac{a}{b} - \frac{c}{d} = \frac{ad-bc}{bd}$

$\frac{4}{5} - \frac{3}{7} = \frac{(4)(7)-(3)(5)}{5 \times 7} = \frac{28-15}{35} = \frac{13}{35}$

SSAT Middle Level Math Prep 2020-2021

Multiplying and Dividing Fractions

✅ Multiplying fractions: multiply the top numbers and multiply the bottom numbers. Simplify if necessary. $\frac{a}{b} \times \frac{c}{d} = \frac{a \times c}{b \times d}$

✅ Dividing fractions: Keep, Change, Flip

Keep first fraction, change division sign to multiplication, and flip the numerator and denominator of the second fraction. Then, solve! $\frac{a}{b} \div \frac{c}{d} = \frac{a}{b} \times \frac{d}{c} = \frac{a \times d}{b \times c}$

Examples:

1) Multiply. $\frac{5}{8} \times \frac{2}{3} =$

   Solution: Multiply the top numbers and multiply the bottom numbers.
   $\frac{5}{8} \times \frac{2}{3} = \frac{5 \times 2}{8 \times 3} = \frac{10}{24}$, simplify: $\frac{10}{24} = \frac{10 \div 2}{24 \div 2} = \frac{5}{12}$

2) Solve. $\frac{1}{3} \div \frac{4}{7} =$

   Solution: Keep first fraction, change division sign to multiplication, and flip the numerator and denominator of the second fraction.
   Then: $\frac{1}{3} \div \frac{4}{7} = \frac{1}{3} \times \frac{7}{4} = \frac{1 \times 7}{3 \times 4} = \frac{7}{12}$

3) Calculate. $\frac{3}{5} \times \frac{2}{3} =$

   Solution: Multiply the top numbers and multiply the bottom numbers.
   $\frac{3}{5} \times \frac{2}{3} = \frac{3 \times 2}{5 \times 3} = \frac{6}{15}$, simplify: $\frac{6}{15} = \frac{6 \div 3}{15 \div 3} = \frac{2}{5}$

4) Solve. $\frac{1}{4} \div \frac{5}{6} =$

   Solution: Keep first fraction, change division sign to multiplication, and flip the numerator and denominator of the second fraction.
   Then: $\frac{1}{4} \div \frac{5}{6} = \frac{1}{4} \times \frac{6}{5} = \frac{1 \times 6}{4 \times 5} = \frac{6}{20}$, simplify: $\frac{6}{20} = \frac{6 \div 2}{20 \div 2} = \frac{3}{10}$

Adding Mixed Numbers

Use following steps for adding mixed numbers:

☑ Add whole numbers of the mixed numbers.

☑ Add the fractions of the mixed numbers.

☑ Find the Least Common Denominator (LCD) if necessary.

☑ Add whole numbers and fractions.

☑ Write your answer in lowest terms.

Examples:

1) Add mixed numbers. $3\frac{1}{3} + 1\frac{4}{5} =$

Solution: Let's rewriting our equation with parts separated, $3\frac{1}{3} + 1\frac{4}{5} = 3 + \frac{1}{3} + 1 + \frac{4}{5}$. Now, add whole number parts: $3 + 1 = 4$

Add the fraction parts $\frac{1}{3} + \frac{4}{5}$. Rewrite to solve with the equivalent fractions. $\frac{1}{3} + \frac{4}{5} = \frac{5}{15} + \frac{12}{15} = \frac{17}{15}$. The answer is an improper fraction (numerator is bigger than denominator). Convert the improper fraction into a mixed number: $\frac{17}{15} = 1\frac{2}{15}$. Now, combine the whole and fraction parts: $4 + 1\frac{2}{15} = 5\frac{2}{15}$

2) Find the sum. $1\frac{2}{5} + 2\frac{1}{2} =$

Solution: Rewriting our equation with parts separated, $1 + \frac{2}{5} + 2 + \frac{1}{2}$. Add the whole number parts:

$1 + 2 = 3$. Add the fraction parts: $\frac{2}{5} + \frac{1}{2} = \frac{4}{10} + \frac{5}{10} = \frac{9}{10}$

Now, combine the whole and fraction parts: $3 + \frac{9}{10} = 3\frac{9}{10}$

SSAT Middle Level Math Prep 2020-2021

Subtract Mixed Numbers

Use the following steps for subtracting mixed numbers.

☑ Convert mixed numbers into improper fractions. $a\frac{c}{b} = \frac{ab+c}{b}$

☑ Find equivalent fractions with the same denominator for unlike fractions. (fractions with different denominators)

☑ Subtract the second fraction from the first one. $\frac{a}{b} - \frac{c}{d} = \frac{ad-bc}{bd}$

☑ Write your answer in lowest terms.

☑ If the answer is an improper fraction, convert it into a mixed number.

Examples:

1) Subtract. $3\frac{4}{5} - 1\frac{3}{4} =$

Solution: Convert mixed numbers into fractions: $3\frac{4}{5} = \frac{3\times5+4}{5} = \frac{19}{5}$ and $1\frac{3}{4} = \frac{1\times4+3}{4} = \frac{7}{4}$
These two fractions are "unlike" fractions. (they have different denominators). Find equivalent fractions with the same denominator. Use this formula: $\frac{a}{b} - \frac{c}{d} = \frac{ad-bc}{bd}$
$\frac{19}{5} - \frac{7}{4} = \frac{(19)(4)-(5)(7)}{5\times4} = \frac{76-35}{20} = \frac{41}{20}$, the answer is an improper fraction, convert it into a mixed number. $\frac{41}{20} = 2\frac{1}{20}$

2) Subtract. $4\frac{3}{8} - 1\frac{1}{2} =$

Solution: Convert mixed numbers into fractions: $4\frac{3}{8} = \frac{4\times8+3}{8} = \frac{35}{8}$ and $1\frac{1}{2} = \frac{1\times2+1}{4} = \frac{3}{2}$
Find equivalent fractions: $\frac{3}{2} = \frac{12}{8}$. Then: $4\frac{3}{8} - 1\frac{1}{2} = \frac{35}{8} - \frac{12}{8} = \frac{23}{8}$
The answer is an improper fraction, convert it into a mixed number.
$$\frac{23}{8} = 2\frac{7}{8}$$

Multiplying Mixed Numbers

Use following steps for multiplying mixed numbers:

☑ Convert the mixed numbers into fractions. $a\frac{c}{b} = a + \frac{c}{b} = \frac{ab+c}{b}$

☑ Multiply fractions. $\frac{a}{b} \times \frac{c}{d} = \frac{a \times c}{b \times d}$

☑ Write your answer in lowest terms.

☑ If the answer is an improper fraction (numerator is bigger than denominator), convert it into a mixed number.

Examples:

1) Multiply. $3\frac{1}{3} \times 4\frac{1}{6} =$

   Solution: Convert mixed numbers into fractions, $3\frac{1}{3} = \frac{3 \times 3 + 1}{3} = \frac{10}{3}$ and $4\frac{1}{6} = \frac{4 \times 6 + 1}{6} = \frac{25}{6}$

   Apply the fractions rule for multiplication, $\frac{10}{3} \times \frac{25}{6} = \frac{10 \times 25}{3 \times 6} = \frac{250}{18}$

   The answer is an improper fraction. Convert it into a mixed number. $\frac{250}{18} = 13\frac{8}{9}$

2) Multiply. $2\frac{1}{2} \times 3\frac{2}{3} =$

   Solution: Converting mixed numbers into fractions, $2\frac{1}{2} \times 3\frac{2}{3} = \frac{5}{2} \times \frac{11}{3}$

   Apply the fractions rule for multiplication, $\frac{5}{2} \times \frac{11}{3} = \frac{5 \times 11}{2 \times 3} = \frac{55}{6} = 9\frac{1}{6}$

3) Multiply mixed numbers. $2\frac{1}{3} \times 2\frac{1}{2} =$

   Solution: Converting mixed numbers to fractions, $2\frac{1}{3} = \frac{7}{3}$ and $2\frac{1}{2} = \frac{5}{2}$. Multiply two fractions:

   $$\frac{7}{3} \times \frac{5}{2} = \frac{7 \times 5}{3 \times 2} = \frac{35}{6} = 5\frac{5}{6}$$

Dividing Mixed Numbers

Use following steps for dividing mixed numbers:

☑ Convert the mixed numbers into fractions. $a\frac{c}{b} = a + \frac{c}{b} = \frac{ab+c}{b}$

☑ Divide fractions: Keep, Change, Flip: Keep first fraction, change division sign to multiplication, and flip the numerator and denominator of the second fraction. Then, solve! $\frac{a}{b} \div \frac{c}{d} = \frac{a}{b} \times \frac{d}{c} = \frac{a \times d}{b \times c}$

☑ Write your answer in lowest terms.

☑ If the answer is an improper fraction (numerator is bigger than denominator), convert it into a mixed number.

Examples:

1) Solve. $3\frac{2}{3} \div 2\frac{1}{2}$

Solution: Convert mixed numbers into fractions: $3\frac{2}{3} = \frac{3 \times 3 + 2}{3} = \frac{11}{3}$ and $2\frac{1}{2} = \frac{2 \times 2 + 1}{2} = \frac{5}{2}$

Keep, Change, Flip: $\frac{11}{3} \div \frac{5}{2} = \frac{11}{3} \times \frac{2}{5} = \frac{11 \times 2}{3 \times 5} = \frac{22}{15}$. The answer is an improper fraction. Convert it into a mixed number: $\frac{22}{15} = 1\frac{7}{15}$

2) Solve. $3\frac{4}{5} \div 1\frac{5}{6}$

Solution: Convert mixed numbers to fractions, then solve:

$3\frac{4}{5} \div 1\frac{5}{6} = \frac{19}{5} \div \frac{11}{6} = \frac{19}{5} \times \frac{6}{11} = \frac{114}{55} = 2\frac{4}{55}$

3) Solve. $2\frac{2}{7} \div 2\frac{3}{5}$

Solution: Converting mixed numbers to fractions: $3\frac{4}{5} \div 1\frac{5}{6} = \frac{16}{7} \div \frac{13}{5}$

Keep, Change, Flip: $\frac{16}{7} \div \frac{13}{5} = \frac{16}{7} \times \frac{5}{13} = \frac{16 \times 5}{7 \times 13} = \frac{80}{91}$

Chapter 1: Practices

✍ *Simplify each fraction.*

1) $\dfrac{18}{30} =$ 3) $\dfrac{35}{55} =$ 5) $\dfrac{54}{81} =$

2) $\dfrac{21}{42} =$ 4) $\dfrac{48}{72} =$ 6) $\dfrac{80}{200} =$

✍ *Find the sum or difference.*

7) $\dfrac{6}{15} + \dfrac{3}{15} =$ 9) $\dfrac{1}{4} + \dfrac{2}{5} =$ 11) $\dfrac{1}{2} - \dfrac{3}{8} =$

8) $\dfrac{2}{3} + \dfrac{1}{9} =$ 10) $\dfrac{7}{10} - \dfrac{3}{10} =$ 12) $\dfrac{5}{7} - \dfrac{3}{5} =$

✍ *Find the answers.*

13) $\dfrac{1}{7} \div \dfrac{3}{8} =$ 15) $\dfrac{5}{7} \times \dfrac{3}{4} =$ *17)* $\dfrac{3}{7} \div \dfrac{5}{8} =$

14) $\dfrac{2}{3} \times \dfrac{4}{7} =$ 16) $\dfrac{2}{5} \div \dfrac{3}{7} =$ *18)* $\dfrac{3}{8} \times \dfrac{4}{7} =$

✍ *Calculate.*

19) $3\dfrac{1}{5} + 2\dfrac{2}{9} =$ 21) $4\dfrac{4}{5} + 1\dfrac{2}{7} =$ 23) $1\dfrac{5}{6} + 1\dfrac{2}{5} =$

20) $1\dfrac{1}{7} + 5\dfrac{2}{5} =$ 22) $2\dfrac{4}{7} + 2\dfrac{3}{5} =$ 24) $3\dfrac{5}{7} + 1\dfrac{2}{9} =$

✍ **Calculate.**

25) $3\frac{2}{5} - 1\frac{2}{9} =$ 27) $4\frac{2}{5} - 2\frac{2}{7} =$ 29) $9\frac{5}{7} - 7\frac{4}{21} =$

26) $5\frac{3}{5} - 1\frac{1}{7} =$ 28) $8\frac{3}{4} - 2\frac{1}{8} =$ 30) $11\frac{7}{12} - 9\frac{5}{6} =$

✍ **Find the answers.**

31) $1\frac{1}{8} \times 1\frac{3}{4} =$ 33) $2\frac{1}{8} \times 1\frac{2}{9} =$ 35) $1\frac{1}{2} \times 5\frac{2}{3} =$

32) $3\frac{1}{5} \times 2\frac{2}{7} =$ 34) $2\frac{3}{8} \times 2\frac{2}{5} =$ 36) $3\frac{1}{2} \times 6\frac{2}{3} =$

✍ **Solve.**

37) $9\frac{1}{2} \div 2\frac{3}{5} =$ 39) $5\frac{3}{4} \div 2\frac{2}{7} =$ 41) $7\frac{2}{5} \div 3\frac{3}{4} =$

38) $2\frac{3}{8} \div 1\frac{2}{5} =$ 40) $8\frac{1}{3} \div 4\frac{1}{4} =$ 42) $2\frac{4}{5} \div 3\frac{2}{3} =$

Answers – Chapter 1

1) $\frac{3}{5}$

2) $\frac{1}{2}$

3) $\frac{7}{11}$

4) $\frac{2}{3}$

5) $\frac{2}{3}$

6) $\frac{2}{5}$

7) $\frac{3}{5}$

8) $\frac{7}{9}$

9) $\frac{13}{20}$

10) $\frac{2}{5}$

11) $\frac{1}{8}$

12) $\frac{4}{35}$

13) $\frac{8}{21}$

14) $\frac{8}{21}$

15) $\frac{15}{28}$

16) $\frac{14}{15}$

17) $\frac{24}{35}$

18) $\frac{3}{14}$

19) $5\frac{19}{45}$

20) $6\frac{19}{35}$

21) $6\frac{3}{35}$

22) $5\frac{6}{35}$

23) $3\frac{7}{30}$

24) $4\frac{59}{63}$

25) $2\frac{8}{45}$

26) $6\frac{16}{35}$

27) $2\frac{4}{35}$

28) $6\frac{5}{8}$

29) $2\frac{11}{21}$

30) $1\frac{3}{4}$

31) $1\frac{31}{32}$

32) $7\frac{11}{35}$

33) $2\frac{43}{72}$

34) $5\frac{7}{10}$

35) $8\frac{1}{2}$

36) $23\frac{1}{3}$

37) $3\frac{17}{26}$

38) $1\frac{39}{56}$

39) $2\frac{33}{64}$

40) $1\frac{49}{51}$

41) $1\frac{73}{75}$

42) $\frac{42}{55}$

Chapter 2:

Decimals

Math Topics that you'll learn in this Chapter:

- ✓ Comparing Decimals

- ✓ Rounding Decimals

- ✓ Adding and Subtracting Decimals

- ✓ Multiplying and Dividing Decimals

Comparing Decimals

- Decimal is a fraction written in a special form. For example, instead of writing $\frac{1}{2}$ you can write 0.5

- A Decimal Number contains a Decimal Point. It separates the whole number part from the fractional part of a decimal number.

- Let's review decimal place values: Example: 53.9861

  5: tens   3: ones   9: tenths

  8: hundredths   6: thousandths   1: tens thousandths

✓ To compare decimals, compare each digit of two decimals in the same place value. Start from left. Compare hundreds, tens, ones, tenth, hundredth, etc.

✓ To compare numbers, use these symbols:

Equal to $=$,   Less than $<$,   Greater than $>$
Greater than or equal $\geq$,   Less than or equal $\leq$

Examples:

1) Compare 0.60 and 0.06.

   Solution: 0.60 *is greater than* 0.06, because the tenth place of 0.60 is 6, but the tenth place of 0.06 is zero. Then: $0.60 > 0.06$

2) Compare 0.0815 and 0.815.

   Solution: 0.815 *is greater than* 0.0815, because the tenth place of 0.815 is 8, but the tenth place of 0.0815 is zero. Then: $0.0815 < 0.815$

Rounding Decimals

☑ We can round decimals to a certain accuracy or number of decimal places. This is used to make calculation easier to do and results easier to understand, when exact values are not too important.

☑ First, you'll need to remember your place values: For example:

$$12.4869$$

1: tens	2: ones	4: tenths
8: hundredths	6: thousandths	9: tens thousandths

☑ To round a decimal, first find the place value you'll round to.

☑ Find the digit to the right of the place value you're rounding to. If it is 5 or bigger, add 1 to the place value you're rounding to and remove all digits on its right side. If the digit to the right of the place value is less than 5, keep the place value and remove all digits on the right.

Examples:

1) Round 1.9278 to the thousandth place value.

   Solution: First look at the next place value to the right, (tens thousandths). It's 8 and it is greater than 5. Thus add 1 to the digit in the thousandth place. Thousandth place is 7. → 7 + 1 = 8, then, the answer is 1.928

2) Round 9.4126 to the nearest hundredth.

   Solution: First look at the digit to the right of hundredth (thousandths place value). It's 2 and it is less than 5, thus remove all the digits to the right of hundredth place. Then, the answer is 9.41

Adding and Subtracting Decimals

☑ Line up the decimal numbers.

☑ Add zeros to have same number of digits for both numbers if necessary.

☑ Remember your place values: For example:

$$73.5196$$

7: tens   3: ones   5: tenths

1: hundredths   9: thousandths   6: tens thousandths

☑ Add or subtract using column addition or subtraction.

Examples:

1) Add. $1.8 + 3.12$

Solution: First line up the numbers: $\begin{array}{r} 1.8 \\ +3.12 \\ \hline \end{array}$ → Add a zero to have same number of digits for

both numbers. $\begin{array}{r} 1.80 \\ +3.12 \\ \hline \end{array}$ → Start with the hundredths place: $0 + 2 = 2$, $\begin{array}{r} 1.80 \\ +3.12 \\ \hline 2 \end{array}$ → Continue

with tenths place: $8 + 1 = 9$, $\begin{array}{r} 1.80 \\ +3.12 \\ \hline .92 \end{array}$ → Add the ones place: $3 + 1 = 4$, $\begin{array}{r} 1.80 \\ +3.12 \\ \hline 4.92 \end{array}$

2) Find the difference. $3.67 - 2.23$

Solution: First line up the numbers: $\begin{array}{r} 3.67 \\ -2.23 \\ \hline \end{array}$ → Start with the hundredths place: $7 - 3 = 4$,

$\begin{array}{r} 3.67 \\ -2.23 \\ \hline 4 \end{array}$ → Continue with tenths place. $6 - 2 = 4$, $\begin{array}{r} 3.67 \\ -2.23 \\ \hline .44 \end{array}$ → Subtract the ones place. $3 - 2 = 1$,

$\begin{array}{r} 3.67 \\ -2.23 \\ \hline 1.44 \end{array}$

Multiplying and Dividing Decimals

For multiplying decimals:

☑ Ignore the decimal point and set up and multiply the numbers as you do with whole numbers.

☑ Count the total number of decimal places in both of the factors.

☑ Place the decimal point in the product.

For dividing decimals:

☑ If the divisor is not a whole number, move decimal point to right to make it a whole number. Do the same for dividend.

☑ Divide similar to whole numbers.

Examples:

1) Find the product. $0.81 \times 0.32 =$

   Solution: Set up and multiply the numbers as you do with whole numbers. Line up the numbers: $\begin{array}{r} 81 \\ \times 32 \end{array}$ → Start with the ones place then continue with other digits → $\frac{\begin{array}{r} 81 \\ \times 32 \end{array}}{2,592}$. Count the total number of decimal places in both of the factors. There are four decimals digits. (two for each factor 0.81 and 0.32) Then: $0.81 \times 0.32 = 0.2592$

2) Find the quotient. $1.60 \div 0.4 =$

   Solution: The divisor is not a whole number. Multiply it by 10 to get 4: → $0.4 \times 10 = 4$

   Do the same for the dividend to get 16. → $1.60 \times 10 = 1.6$

   Now, divide: $16 \div 4 = 4$. The answer is 4.

Chapter 2: Practices

✎ *Compare. Use >, =, and <*

1) $0.88 \ \square \ 0.088$

2) $0.56 \ \square \ 0.57$

3) $0.99 \ \square \ 0.89$

4) $1.55 \ \square \ 1.65$

5) $1.58 \ \square \ 1.75$

6) $2.91 \ \square \ 2.85$

✎ *Round each decimal to the nearest whole number.*

7) 5.94

8) 16.47

9) 9.7

10) 35.8

11) 24.46

12) 12.5

✎ *Find the sum or difference.*

13) $43.15 + 23.65 =$

14) $56.74 - 22.43 =$

15) $25.47 + 31.76 =$

16) $69.87 - 35.98 =$

17) $45.53 + 18.95 =$

18) $25.13 - 18.72 =$

✎ *Find the product and quotient.*

19) $0.5 \times 0.8 =$

20) $6.4 \div 0.4 =$

21) $3.25 \times 2.2 =$

22) $8.4 \div 2.5 =$

23) $5.4 \times 0.6 =$

24) $1.42 \div 0.5 =$

Answers – Chapter 2

1) 0.88 > 0.088
2) 0.56 < 0.57
3) 0.99 > 0.89
4) 1.55 < 1.65
5) 1.58 < 1.75
6) 2.91 > 2.85
7) 6
8) 16
9) 10
10) 36
11) 24
12) 13

13) 66.8
14) 34.31
15) 57.23
16) 33.89
17) 64.48
18) 6.41
19) 0.4
20) 16
21) 7.15
22) 3.36
23) 3.24
24) 2.84

Chapter 3:

Integers and Order of Operations

Math Topics that you'll learn in this Chapter:

- ✓ Adding and Subtracting Integers

- ✓ Multiplying and Dividing Integers

- ✓ Order of Operations

- ✓ Integers and Absolute Value

Adding and Subtracting Integers

☑ Integers include: zero, counting numbers, and the negative of the counting numbers. $\{... , -3, -2, -1, 0, 1, 2, 3, ...\}$

☑ Add a positive integer by moving to the right on the number line. (you will get a bigger number)

☑ Add a negative integer by moving to the left on the number line. (you will get a smaller number)

☑ Subtract an integer by adding its opposite.

Examples:

1) Solve. $(-4) - (-5) =$

Solution: Keep the first number and convert the sign of the second number to its opposite. (change subtraction into addition. Then: $(-4) + 5 = 1$

2) Solve. $11 + (8 - 19) =$

Solution: First subtract the numbers in brackets, $8 - 19 = -11$.

Then: $11 + (-11) = \rightarrow$ change addition into subtraction: $11 - 11 = 0$

3) Solve. $5 - (-14 - 3) =$

Solution: First subtract the numbers in brackets, $-14 - 3 = -17$

Then: $5 - (-17) = \rightarrow$ change subtraction into addition: $5 + 17 = 22$

4) Solve. $10 + (-6 - 15) =$

Solution: First subtract the numbers in brackets, $-6 - 15 = -21$

Then: $10 + (-21) = \rightarrow$ change addition into subtraction: $10 - 21 = -11$

Multiplying and Dividing Integers

Use following rules for multiplying and dividing integers:

☑ (negative) × (negative) = positive

☑ (negative) ÷ (negative) = positive

☑ (negative) × (positive) = negative

☑ (negative) ÷ (positive) = negative

☑ (positive) × (positive) = positive

☑ (positive) ÷ (negative) = negative

Examples:

1) Solve. $2 \times (-3) =$

Solution: Use this rule: (positive) × (negative) = negative.
Then: $(2) \times (-3) = -6$

2) Solve. $(-5) + (-27 \div 9) =$

Solution: First divided -27 by 9 , the numbers in brackets, use this rule:
(negative) ÷ (positive) = negative. Then: $-27 \div 9 = -3$
$(-5) + (-27 \div 9) = (-5) + (-3) = -5 - 3 = -8$

3) Solve. $(15 - 17) \times (-8) =$

Solution: First subtract the numbers in brackets, $15 - 17 = -2 \rightarrow (-2) \times (-8) =$

Now use this rule: (negative) × (negative) = positive
$(-2) \times (-8) = 16$

4) Solve. $(16 - 10) \div (-2) =$

Solution: First subtract the numbers in brackets, $16 - 10 = 6 \rightarrow (6) \div (-2) =$

Now use this rule: (positive) ÷ (negative) = negative
$(6) \div (-2) = -3$

Order of Operations

☑ In Mathematics, "operations" are addition, subtraction, multiplication, division, exponentiation (written as b^n), and grouping;

☑ When there is more than one math operation in an expression, use PEMDAS: (to memorize this rule, remember the phrase "Please Excuse My Dear Aunt Sally".)

- ❖ Parentheses
- ❖ Exponents
- ❖ Multiplication and Division (from left to right)
- ❖ Addition and Subtraction (from left to right)

Examples:

1) Calculate. $(3 + 5) \div (3^2 \div 9) =$

   Solution: First simplify inside parentheses: $(8) \div (9 \div 9) = (8) \div (1)$, Then: $(8) \div (1) = 8$

2) Solve. $(7 \times 8) - (12 - 4) =$

   Solution: First calculate within parentheses: $(7 \times 8) - (12 - 4) = (56) - (8)$, Then: $(56) - (8) = 48$

3) Calculate. $-2[(8 \times 9) \div (2^2 \times 2)] =$

   Solution: First calculate within parentheses: $-2[(72) \div (4 \times 2)] = -2[(72) \div (8)] = -2[9]$ multiply -2 and 9. Then: $-2[9] = -18$

4) Solve. $(14 \div 7) + (-13 + 8) =$

   Solution: First calculate within parentheses: $(14 \div 7) + (-13 + 8) = (2) + (-5)$

   Then: $(2) - (5) = -3$

Integers and Absolute Value

✓ The absolute value of a number is its distance from zero, in either direction, on the number line. For example, the distance of 9 and -9 from zero on number line is 9.

✓ The absolute value of an integer is the numerical value without its sign. (negative or positive)

✓ The vertical bar is used for absolute value as in $|x|$.

✓ The absolute value of a number is never negative; because it only shows, "how far the number is from zero".

Examples:

1) Calculate. $|12 - 4| \times 4 =$

   Solution: First solve $|12 - 4|$, $\rightarrow |12 - 4| = |8|$, the absolute value of 8 is 8, $|8| = 8$
   Then: $8 \times 4 = 32$

2) Solve. $\frac{|-16|}{4} \times |3 - 8| =$

   Solution: First find $|-16|$, $\rightarrow$ the absolute value of -16 is 16, then: $|-16| = 16$,
   $\frac{16}{4} \times |3 - 8| =$
   Now, calculate $|3 - 8|$, $\rightarrow |3 - 8| = |-5|$, the absolute value of -5 is 5. $|-5| = 5$
   Then: $\frac{16}{4} \times 5 = 4 \times 5 = 20$

3) Solve. $|9 - 3| \times \frac{|-3 \times 8|}{6} =$

   Solution: First calculate $|9 - 3|$, $\rightarrow |9 - 3| = |6|$, the absolute value of 6 is 6, $|6| = 6$. Then:
   $6 \times \frac{|-3 \times 8|}{6}$
   Now calculate $|-3 \times 8|$, $\rightarrow |-3 \times 8| = |-24|$, the absolute value of -24 is 24, $|-24| = 24$
   Then: $6 \times \frac{24}{6} = 6 \times 4 = 24$

Chapter 3: Practices

✍ *Find each sum or difference.*

1) $18 + (-5) =$

2) $(-16) + 24 =$

3) $(-12) + (-9) =$

4) $14 + (-8) + 6 =$

5) $24 + (-10 - 7) =$

6) $(-15) + (-6 + 12) =$

✍ *Find each product or quotient.*

7) $8 \times (-6) =$

8) $(-12) \div (-3) =$

9) $(-4) \times (-7) \times 2 =$

10) $3 \times (-5) \times (-6) =$

11) $(-7 - 37) \div (-11) =$

12) $(8 - 6) \times (-24) =$

✍ *Evaluate each expression.*

13) $8 + (3 \times 7) =$

14) $(18 \times 2) - 14 =$

15) $(15 - 7) + (2 \times 6) =$

16) $(8 + 4) \div (2^3 \div 2) =$

17) $2[(6 \times 3) \div (3^2 \times 2)] =$

18) $-3[(8 \times 2^2) \div (8 \times 2)] =$

✍ *Find the answers.*

19) $|-6| + |9 - 12| =$

20) $|8| - |7 - 19| + 1 =$

21) $\frac{|-40|}{8} \times \frac{|-15|}{5} =$

22) $|7 \times -5| \times \frac{|-32|}{8} =$

23) $\frac{|-121|}{11} - |-8 \times 2| =$

24) $\frac{|-3 \times -6|}{9} \times \frac{|4 \times -6|}{8} =$

Answers – Chapter 3

1) 13
2) 8
3) −21
4) 12
5) 7
6) −9
7) −48
8) 4
9) 56
10) 90
11) 4
12) −48

13) 29
14) 22
15) 20
16) 3
17) 2
18) −6
19) 9
20) −3
21) 15
22) 140
23) −5
24) 6

Chapter 4:

Ratios and Proportions

Math Topics that you'll learn in this Chapter:

- ✓ Simplifying Ratios
- ✓ Proportional Ratios
- ✓ Similarity and Ratios

Simplifying Ratios

✓ Ratios are used to make comparisons between two numbers.

✓ Ratios can be written as a fraction, using the word "to", or with a colon. Example: $\frac{3}{4}$ or "3 to 4" or 3:4

✓ You can calculate equivalent ratios by multiplying or dividing both sides of the ratio by the same number.

Examples:

1) Simplify. $9:3 =$

   Solution: Both numbers 9 and 3 are divisible by 3 , $\Rightarrow 9 \div 3 = 3$, $3 \div 3 = 1$, Then: $9:3 = 3:1$

2) Simplify. $\frac{24}{44} =$

   Solution: Both numbers 24 and 44 are divisible by 4, $\Rightarrow 24 \div 4 = 6$, $44 \div 4 = 11$, Then: $\frac{24}{44} = \frac{6}{11}$

3) There are 36 students in a class and 16 of them are girls. Write the ratio of girls to boys.

   Solution: Subtract 16 from 36 to find the number of boys in the class. $36 - 16 = 20$. There are 20 boys in the class. So, ratio of girls to boys is $16:20$. Now, simplify this ratio. Both 20 and 16 are divisible by 4. Then: $20 \div 4 = 5$, and $16 \div 4 = 4$. In simplest form, this ratio is $4:5$

4) A recipe calls for butter and sugar in the ratio $3:4$. If you're using 9 cups of butter, how many cups of sugar should you use?

   Solution: Since, you use 9 cups of butter, or 3 times as much, you need to multiply the amount of sugar by 3. Then: $4 \times 3 = 12$. So, you need to use 12 cups of sugar. You can solve this using equivalent fractions: $\frac{3}{4} = \frac{9}{12}$

34

Proportional Ratios

- ☑ Two ratios are proportional if they represent the same relationship.

- ☑ A proportion means that two ratios are equal. It can be written in two ways: $\frac{a}{b} = \frac{c}{d}$ $a : b = c : d$

- ☑ The proportion $\frac{a}{b} = \frac{c}{d}$ can be written as: $a \times d = c \times b$

Examples:

1) Solve this proportion for x. $\frac{3}{7} = \frac{12}{x}$

    Solution: Use cross multiplication: $\frac{3}{7} = \frac{12}{x} \Rightarrow 3 \times x = 7 \times 12 \Rightarrow 3x = 84$

    Divide both sides by 3 to find x: $x = \frac{84}{3} \Rightarrow x = 28$

2) If a box contains red and blue balls in ratio of $3 : 7$ red to blue, how many red balls are there if 49 blue balls are in the box?

    Solution: Write a proportion and solve. $\frac{3}{7} = \frac{x}{49}$

    Use cross multiplication: $3 \times 49 = 7 \times x \Rightarrow 147 = 7x$

    Divide to find x: $x = \frac{147}{7} \Rightarrow x = 21$. There are 21 red balls in the box.

3) Solve this proportion for x. $\frac{2}{9} = \frac{12}{x}$

    Solution: Use cross multiplication: $\frac{2}{9} = \frac{12}{x} \Rightarrow 2 \times x = 9 \times 12 \Rightarrow 2x = 108$

    Divide to find x: $x = \frac{108}{2} \Rightarrow x = 54$

4) Solve this proportion for x. $\frac{6}{7} = \frac{18}{x}$

    Solution: Use cross multiplication: $\frac{6}{7} = \frac{18}{x} \Rightarrow 6 \times x = 7 \times 18 \Rightarrow 6x = 126$

    Divide to find x: $x = \frac{126}{6} \Rightarrow x = 21$

Similarity and Ratios

✓ Two figures are similar if they have the same shape.

✓ Two or more figures are similar if the corresponding angles are equal, and the corresponding sides are in proportion.

Examples:

1) Following triangles are similar. What is the value of unknown side?

Solution: Find the corresponding sides and write a proportion.

$\frac{5}{10} = \frac{4}{x}$. Now, use cross product to solve for x:

$\frac{5}{10} = \frac{4}{x} \rightarrow 5 \times x = 10 \times 4 \rightarrow 5x = 40$. Divide

both sides by 5. Then: $5x = 40 \rightarrow \frac{5x}{5} = \frac{40}{5} \rightarrow x = 8$

The missing side is 8.

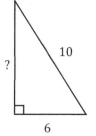 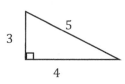

2) Two rectangles are similar. The first is 6 feet wide and 20 feet long. The second is 15 feet wide. What is the length of the second rectangle?

Solution: Let's put x for the length of the second rectangle. Since two rectangles are similar, their corresponding sides are in proportion. Write a proportion and solve for the missing number. $\frac{6}{15} = \frac{20}{x} \rightarrow 6x = 15 \times 20 \rightarrow 6x = 300 \rightarrow x = \frac{300}{6} = 50$

The length of the second rectangle is 50 feet.

Chapter 4: Practices

🖎 *Reduce each ratio.*

1) $9:18 = $ ___ : ___

2) $6:54 = $ ___ : ___

3) $28:49 = $ ___ : ___

4) Bob has 12 red cards and 20 green cards. What is the ratio of Bob's red cards to his green cards? _____

5) In a party, 10 soft drinks are required for every 12 guests. If there are 252 guests, how many soft drinks is required? _____

6) In Jack's class, 18 of the students are tall and 10 are short. In Michael's class 54 students are tall and 30 students are short. Which class has a higher ratio of tall to short students? _____

🖎 *Solve each proportion.*

7) $\frac{3}{7} = \frac{18}{x}, x = $ ____

8) $\frac{5}{9} = \frac{x}{108}, x = $ ____

9) $\frac{2}{13} = \frac{8}{x}, x = $ ____

10) $\frac{4}{10} = \frac{6}{x}, x = $ ____

11) $\frac{8}{20} = \frac{x}{65}, x = $ ____

12) $\frac{6}{15} = \frac{14}{x}, x = $ ____

🖎 *Solve each problem.*

13) Two rectangles are similar. The first is $8\ feet$ wide and $22\ feet$ long. The second is $12\ feet$ wide. What is the length of the second rectangle? _____

14) Two rectangles are similar. One is $3.2\ meters$ by $8\ meters$. The longer side of the second rectangle is $34.5\ meters$. What is the other side of the second rectangle? _____

Answers – Chapter 4

1) 1 : 2
2) 1 : 9
3) 4 : 7
4) 3 : 5
5) 210
6) The ratio for both classes is 9 to 5.
7) 42

8) 60
9) 52
10) 15
11) 26
12) 35
13) 33 feet
14) 13.8 meters

Chapter 5:

Percentage

Math Topics that you'll learn in this Chapter:

✓ Percentage Calculations

✓ Percent Problems

✓ Percent of Increase and Decrease

✓ Discount, Tax and Tip

✓ Simple Interest

Percent Problems

☑ Percent is a ratio of a number and 100. It always has the same denominator, 100. Percent symbol is "%".

☑ Percent means "per 100". So, 20% is 20/100.

☑ In each percent problem, we are looking for the base, or part or the percent.

☑ Use the following equations to find each missing section in a percent problem:

- Base = Part ÷ Percent
- Part = Percent × Base
- Percent = Part ÷ Base

Examples:

1) What is 25% of 60?

Solution: In this problem, we have percent (25%) and base (60) and we are looking for the "part".

Use this formula: $part = percent \times base$. Then: $part = 25\% \times 60 = \frac{25}{100} \times 60 = 0.25 \times 60 = 15$.

The answer:

25% of 60 is 15.

2) 20 is what percent of 400?

Solution: In this problem, we are looking for the percent. Use this equation:

$Percent = Part \div Base \rightarrow Percent = 20 \div 400 = 0.05 = 5\%$.

Then: 20 is 5 percent of 400.

Percent of Increase and Decrease

☑ Percent of change (increase or decrease) is a mathematical concept that represents the degree of change over time.

☑ To find the percentage of increase or decrease:

1. New Number – Original Number

2. The result ÷ Original Number × 100

☑ Or use this formula: Percent of change = $\frac{new\ number - original\ number}{original\ number} \times 100$

☑ Note: If your answer is a negative number, then this is a percentage decrease. If it is positive, then this is a percentage increase.

Examples:

1) The price of a shirt increases from $20 to $30. What is the percentage increase?
   Solution: First find the difference: $30 - 20 = 10$
   Then: $10 \div 20 \times 100 = \frac{10}{20} \times 100 = 50$. The percentage increase is 50. It means that the price of the shirt increased 50%.

2) The price of a table increased from $25 to $40. What is the percent of increase?
   Solution: Use percentage formula: $Percent\ of\ change = \frac{new\ number - original\ number}{original\ number} \times$
   $100 = \frac{40-25}{25} \times 100 = \frac{15}{25} \times 100 = 0.6 \times 100 = 60$. The percentage increase is 60. It means that the price of the table increased 60%.

3) The population of a town was 50,000 in the 2000 census and 40,000 in the 2010 census. By what percent did the population decrease?
   Solution: Use percentage formula:
   $Percent\ of\ change = \frac{new\ number - original\ number}{original\ number} \times 100 = \frac{40,000 - 50,000}{50,000} \times 100 = \frac{-10,000}{50,000} \times$
   $100 = -0.2 \times 100 = -20$. The population of the town decreased by 20%.

Discount, Tax and Tip

- ☑ To find discount: Multiply the regular price by the rate of discount
- ☑ To find selling price: Original price – discount
- ☑ To find tax: Multiply the tax rate to the taxable amount (income, property value, etc.)
- ☑ To find tip, multiply the rate to the selling price.

Examples:

1) With an 10% discount, Ella was able to save $45 on a dress. What was the original price of the dress?

   Solution: let x be the original price of the dress. Then: $10\% \ of \ x = 45$. Write an equation and solve for x: $0.10 \times x = 45 \rightarrow x = \frac{45}{0.10} = 450$. The original price of the dress was $450.

2) Sophia purchased a new computer for a price of $950 at the Apple Store. What is the total amount her credit card is charged if the sales tax is 7%?

   Solution: The taxable amount is $950, and the tax rate is 7%. Then: $Tax = 0.07 \times 950 = 66.50$

   $Final \ price = Selling \ price + Tax \rightarrow final \ price = \$950 + \$66.50 = \$1,016.50$

3) Nicole and her friends went out to eat at a restaurant. If their bill was $80.00 and they gave their server a 15% tip, how much did they pay altogether?

   Solution: First find the tip. To find tip, multiply the rate to the bill amount.

   $Tip = 80 \times 0.15 = 12$. The final price is: $\$80 + \$12 = \$92$

Simple Interest

☑ Simple Interest: The charge for borrowing money or the return for lending it.

☑ Simple interest is calculated on the initial amount (principal).

☑ To solve a simple interest problem, use this formula:

Interest = principal x rate x time $(I = p \times r \times t = prt)$

Examples:

1) Find simple interest for $300 investment at 6% for 5 years.

   Solution: Use Interest formula: $I = prt$ $(P = \$300, r = 6\% = \frac{6}{100} = 0.06$ and $t = 5)$
   Then: $I = 300 \times 0.06 \times 5 = \$90$

2) Find simple interest for $1,600 at 5% for 2 years.

   Solution: Use Interest formula: $I = prt$ $(P = \$1,600, r = 5\% = \frac{5}{100} = 0.05$ and $t = 2)$
   Then: $I = 1,600 \times 0.05 \times 2 = \$160$

3) Andy received a student loan to pay for his educational expenses this year. What is the interest on the loan if he borrowed $6,500 at 8% for 6 years?
   Solution: Use Interest formula: $I = prt$. $P = \$6,500, r = 8\% = 0.08$ and $t = 6$

   Then: $I = 6,500 \times 0.08 \times 8 = \$3,120$

4) Bob is starting his own small business. He borrowed $10,000 from the bank at a 6% rate for 6 months. Find the interest Bob will pay on this loan.
   Solution: Use Interest formula: $I = prt$. $P = \$10,000, r = 6\% = 0.06$ and $t = 0.5$ (6 months is half year). Then: $I = 10,000 \times 0.06 \times 0.5 = \$300$

Chapter 5: Practices

✎ *Solve each problem.*

1) 15 is what percent of 60? ____%

2) 18 is what percent of 24? ____%

3) 25 is what percent of 500? ____%

4) 14 is what percent of 280? ____%

5) 45 is what percent of 180? ____%

6) 70 is what percent of 350? ____%

✎ *Solve each percent of change word problem.*

7) Bob got a raise, and his hourly wage increased from $15 to $18. What is the percent increase? _____ %

8) The price of a pair of shoes increases from $40 to $66. What is the percent increase? ____ %

9) At a coffeeshop, the price of a cup of coffee increased from $1.20 to $1.44. What is the percent increase in the cost of the coffee? _____ %

✎ *Find the selling price of each item.*

10) Original price of a computer: $650

Tax: 8%, Selling price: $_____

11) Original price of a laptop: $480

Tax: 15%, Selling price: $_____

12) Nicolas hired a moving company. The company charged $400 for its services, and Nicolas gives the movers a 15% tip. How much does Nicolas tip the movers? $_____

13) Mason has lunch at a restaurant and the cost of his meal is $30. Mason wants to leave a 20% tip. What is Mason's total bill including tip? $_____

✍ *Determine the simple interest for these loans.*

14) $440 *at* 5% *for* 6 *years.* $___

15) $460 *at* 2.5% *for* 4 *years.* $__

16) $500 *at* 3% *for* 5 *years.* $___

17) $550 at 9% for 2 years. $___

18) A new car, valued at $28,000, depreciates at 9% per year. What is the value of the car one year after purchase? $_____

19) Sara puts $4,000 into an investment yielding 5% annual simple interest; she left the money in for five years. How much interest does Sara get at the end of those five years? $_____

Answers – Chapter 5

1) 25%
2) 75%
3) 5%
4) 5%
5) 25%
6) 20%
7) 20%
8) 65%
9) 20%
10) $702.00

11) $552.00
12) $60.00
13) $36.00
14) $132
15) $46
16) $75
17) $99
18) $25,480.00
19) $1,000.00

Chapter 6:

Expressions and Variables

Math Topics that you'll learn in this Chapter:

- ✓ Simplifying Variable Expressions
- ✓ Simplifying Polynomial Expressions
- ✓ The Distributive Property
- ✓ Evaluating One Variable
- ✓ Evaluating Two Variables

Simplifying Variable Expressions

☑ In algebra, a variable is a letter used to stand for a number. The most common letters are: $x, y, z, a, b, c, m, and\ n$.

☑ Algebraic expression is an expression contains integers, variables, and the math operations such as addition, subtraction, multiplication, division, etc.

☑ In an expression, we can combine "like" terms. (values with same variable and same power)

Examples:

1) Simplify. $(2x + 3x + 4) =$

   Solution: In this expression, there are three terms: $2x, 3x$, and 4. Two terms are "like terms": $2x$ and $3x$. Combine like terms. $2x + 3x = 5x$. Then: $(2x + 3x + 4) = 5x + 4$

   (remember you cannot combine variables and numbers.)

2) Simplify. $12 - 3x^2 + 5x + 4x^2 =$

   Solution: Combine "like" terms: $-3x^2 + 4x^2 = x^2$. Then:

   $12 - 3x^2 + 5x + 4x^2 = 12 + x^2 + 5x$. Write in standard form (biggest powers first):

   $12 + x^2 + 5x = x^2 + 5x + 12$

3) Simplify. $(10x^2 + 2x^2 + 3x) =$

   Solution: Combine like terms. Then: $(10x^2 + 2x^2 + 3x) = 12x^2 + 3x$

4) Simplify. $15x - 3x^2 + 9x + 5x^2 =$

   Solution: Combine "like" terms: $15x + 9x = 24x$, and $-3x^2 + 5x^2 = 2x^2$

   Then: $15x - 3x^2 + 9x + 5x^2 = 24x + 2x^2$. Write in standard form (biggest powers first): $24x + 2x^2 = 2x^2 + 24x$

SSAT Middle Level Math Prep 2020-2021

Simplifying Polynomial Expressions

☑️   In mathematics, a polynomial is an expression consisting of variables and coefficients that involves only the operations of addition, subtraction, multiplication, and non-negative integer exponents of variables. $P(x) = a_n x^n + a_{n-1} x^{n-1} + \ldots + a_2 x^2 + a_1 x + a_0$

☑️   Polynomials must always be simplified as much as possible. It means you must add together any like terms. (values with same variable and same power)

Examples:

1) Simplify this Polynomial Expressions. $x^2 - 5x^3 + 2x^4 - 4x^3$

   Solution: Combine "like" terms: $-5x^3 - 4x^3 = -9x^3$

   Then: $x^2 - 5x^3 + 2x^4 - 4x^3 = x^2 - 9x^3 + 2x^4$

   Now, write the expression in standard form: $2x^4 - 9x^3 + x^2$

2) Simplify this expression. $(2x^2 - x^3) - (x^3 - 4x^2) =$

   Solution: First use distributive property: $\rightarrow$ multiply $(-)$ into $(x^3 - 4x^2)$

   $(2x^2 - x^3) - (x^3 - 4x^2) = 2x^2 - x^3 - x^3 + 4x^2$

   Then combine "like" terms: $2x^2 - x^3 - x^3 + 4x^2 = 6x^2 - 2x^3$

   And write in standard form: $6x^2 - 2x^3 = -2x^3 + 6x^2$

3) Simplify. $4x^4 - 5x^3 + 15x^4 - 12x^3 =$

   Solution: Combine "like" terms: $-5x^3 - 12x^3 = -17x^3$ and $4x^4 + 15x^4 = 19x^4$

   Then: $4x^4 - 5x^3 + 15x^4 - 12x^3 = 19x^4 - 17x^3$

The Distributive Property

- The distributive property (or the distributive property of multiplication over addition and subtraction) simplifies and solves expressions in the form of: $a(b + c)$ or $a(b - c)$
- The distributive property is multiplying a term outside the parentheses by the terms inside.
- Distributive Property rule: $a(b + c) = ab + ac$

Examples:

1) *Simply using distributive property.* $(-4)(x - 5)$

   Solution: Use Distributive Property rule: $a(b + c) = ab + ac$

   $(-4)(x - 5) = (-4 \times x) + (-4) \times (-5) = -4x + 20$

2) *Simply.* $(3)(2x - 4)$

   Solution: Use Distributive Property rule: $a(b + c) = ab + ac$

   $(3)(2x - 4) = (3 \times 2x) + (3) \times (-4) = 6x - 12$

3) *Simply.* $(-3)(3x - 5) + 4x$

   Solution: First, simplify $(-3)(3x - 5)$ using distributive property.

   Then: $(-3)(3x - 5) = -9x + 15$

   Now combine like terms: $(-3)(3x - 5) + 4x = -9x + 15 + 4x$

   In this expression, $-9x$ and $4x$ are "like terms" and we can combine them.

   $-9x + 4x = -5x$. Then: $-9x + 15 + 4x = -5x + 15$

Evaluating One Variable

✓ To evaluate one variable expressions, find the variable and substitute a number for that variable.

✓ Perform the arithmetic operations.

Examples:

1) *Calculate this expression for* $x = 3$. $15 - 3x$

   Solution: First substitute 3 for x

   Then: $15 - 3x = 15 - 3(3)$

   Now, use order of operation to find the answer: $15 - 3(3) = 15 - 9 = 6$

2) *Evaluate this expression for* $x = 1$. $5x - 12$

   Solution: First substitute 1 for x, then:

   $5x - 12 = 5(1) - 12$

   Now, use order of operation to find the answer: $5(1) - 12 = 5 - 12 = -7$

3) *Find the value of this expression when* $x = 5$. $25 - 4x$

   Solution: First substitute 5 for x, then:

   $25 - 4x = 25 - 4(5) = 25 - 20 = 5$

4) *Solve this expression for* $x = -2$. $12 + 3x$

   Solution: Substitute -2 for x, then: $12 + 3x = 12 + 3(-2) = 12 - 6 = 6$

Evaluating Two Variables

☑ To evaluate an algebraic expression, substitute a number for each variable.

☑ Perform the arithmetic operations to find the value of the expression.

Examples:

1) *Calculate this expression for* $a = 3$ *and* $b = -2$. $3a - 6b$

   Solution: First substitute 3 for a, and -2 for b , then:

   $$3a - 6b = 3(3) - 6(-2)$$

   Now, use order of operation to find the answer: $3(3) - 6(-2) = 9 + 12 = 21$

2) *Evaluate this expression for* $x = 3$ *and* $y = 1$. $3x + 5y$

   Solution: Substitute 3 for x, and 1 for y , then:

   $$3x + 5y = 3(3) + 5(1) = 9 + 5 = 14$$

3) *Find the value of this expression when* $a = 1$ *and* $b = 2$. $5(3a - 2b)$

   Solution: Substitute 1 for a, and 2 for b , then:

   $$5(3a - 2b) = 15a - 10b = 15(1) - 10(2) = 15 - 20 = -5$$

4) *Solve this expression.* $4x - 3y$, $x = 3$, $y = 5$

   Solution: Substitute 3 for x, and 5 for y and simplify. Then: $4x - 3y = 4(3) - 3(5) = 12 - 15 = -3$

Chapter 6: Practices

✎ **Simplify each expression.**

1) $(6x - 4x + 8 + 6) =$

2) $(-14x + 26x - 12) =$

3) $(24x - 6 - 18x + 3) =$

4) $5 + 8x^2 - 9 =$

5) $7x - 4x^2 + 6x =$

6) $15x^2 - 3x - 6x^2 + 4 =$

✎ **Simplify each polynomial.**

7) $2x^2 + 5x^3 - 7x^2 + 12x =$ _____

8) $2x^4 - 5x^5 + 8x^4 - 8x^2 =$ _____

9) $5x^3 + 15x - x^2 - 2x^3 =$ _____

10) $(8x^3 - 6x^2) + (9x^2 - 10x) =$ _____

11) $(12x^4 + 4x^3) - (8x^3 - 2x^4) =$ _____

12) $(9x^5 - 7x^3) - (5x^3 + x^2) =$ _____

✎ **Use the distributive property to simply each expression.**

13) $4(5 + 6x) =$

14) $5(8 - 4x) =$

15) $(-6)(2 - 9x) =$

16) $(-7)(6x - 4) =$

17) $(3x + 12)4 =$

18) $(8x - 5)(-3) =$

✎ **Evaluate each expression using the value given.**

19) $8 - x, x = -3$

20) $x + 12, x = -6$

21) $5x - 3, x = 2$

22) $4 - 6x, x = 1$

23) $3x + 1, x = -2$

24) $15 - 2x, x = 5$

✎ *Evaluate each expression using the values given.*

25) $4x - 2y, \ x = 4, y = -2$

26) $6a + 3b, \ a = 2, b = 4$

27) $12x - 5y - 8, \ x = 2, y = 3$

28) $-7a + 3b + 9, \ a = 4, b = 6$

29) $2x + 14 + 4y, \ x = 6, y = 8$

30) $4a - (5a - b) + 5, a = 4, b = 6$

Answers – Chapter 6

1) $2x + 14$
2) $12x - 12$
3) $6x - 3$
4) $8x^2 - 4$
5) $-4x^2 + 13x$
6) $9x^2 - 3x + 4$

7) $5x^3 - 5x^2 + 12x$
8) $-5x^5 + 10x^4 - 8x^2$
9) $3x^3 - x^2 + 15x$
10) $8x^3 + 3x^2 - 10x$
11) $14x^4 - 4x^3$
12) $9x^5 - 12x^3 - x^2$

13) $24x + 20$
14) $-20x + 40$
15) $54x - 12$
16) $-42x + 28$
17) $12x + 48$
18) $-24x + 15$

19) 11
20) 6
21) 7
22) -2
23) -5
24) 5

25) 20
26) 24
27) 1
28) -1
29) 58
30) 7

Chapter 7:

Equations and Inequalities

Math Topics that you'll learn in this Chapter:

- ✓ One–Step Equations

- ✓ Multi–Step Equations

- ✓ System of Equations

- ✓ Graphing Single–Variable Inequalities

- ✓ One–Step Inequalities

- ✓ Multi–Step Inequalities

One–Step Equations

- ☑ The values of two expressions on both sides of an equation are equal. Example: $ax = b$. In this equation, ax is equal to b.

- ☑ Solving an equation means finding the value of the variable.

- ☑ You only need to perform one Math operation in order to solve the one-step equations.

- ☑ To solve one-step equation, find the inverse (opposite) operation is being performed.

- ☑ The inverse operations are:

- Addition and subtraction
- Multiplication and division

Examples:

1) *Solve this equation for x.* $3x = 18, x = ?$

   Solution: Here, the operation is multiplication (variable x is multiplied by 3) and its inverse operation is division. To solve this equation, divide both sides of equation by 3:

   $$3x = 18 \rightarrow \frac{3x}{3} = \frac{18}{3} \rightarrow x = 6$$

2) *Solve this equation.* $x + 15 = 0$, $x = ?$

   Solution: In this equation 15 is added to the variable x. The inverse operation of addition is subtraction. To solve this equation, subtract 15 from both sides of the equation: $x + 15 - 15 = 0 - 15$. Then simplify: $x + 15 - 15 = 0 - 15 \rightarrow x = -15$

3) *Solve this equation for x.* $x - 23 = 0$

   Solution: Here, the operation is subtraction and its inverse operation is addition. To solve this equation, add 23 to both sides of the equation: $x + 23 - 23 = 0 - 23 \rightarrow x = -23$

Multi–Step Equations

☑ To solve a multi-step equation, combine "like" terms on one side.

☑ Bring variables to one side by adding or subtracting.

☑ Simplify using the inverse of addition or subtraction.

☑ Simplify further by using the inverse of multiplication or division.

☑ Check your solution by plugging the value of the variable into the original equation.

Examples:

1) *Solve this equation for x.* $3x + 6 = 16 - 2x$

   Solution: First bring variables to one side by adding $2x$ to both sides. Then:

   $3x + 6 = 16 - 2x \rightarrow 3x + 6 + 2x = 16 - 2x + 2x$. Simplify: $5x + 6 = 16$

   Now, subtract 6 from both sides of the equation: $5x + 6 - 6 = 16 - 6 \rightarrow 5x = 10 \rightarrow$

   Divide both sides by 5: $5x = 10 \rightarrow \frac{5x}{5} = \frac{10}{5} \rightarrow x = 2$

   Let's check this solution by substituting the value of 2 for x in the original equation:

   $x = 2 \rightarrow 3x + 6 = 16 - 2x \rightarrow 3(2) + 6 = 16 - 2(2) \rightarrow 6 + 6 = 16 - 4 \rightarrow 12 = 12$

   The answer $x = 2$ is correct.

2) *Solve this equation for x.* $-4x + 4 = 16$

   Solution: Subtract 4 from both sides of the equation. $-4x + 4 - 4 = 16 - 4 \rightarrow -4x = 12$

   Divide both sides by -4, then: $-4x = 12 \rightarrow \frac{-4x}{-4} = \frac{12}{-4} \rightarrow x = -3$

   Now, check the solution: $x = -3 \rightarrow -4x + 4 = 16 \rightarrow -4(-3) + 4 = 16 \rightarrow 16 = 16$

   The answer $x = -2$ is correct.

SSAT Middle Level Math Prep 2020-2021

System of Equations

☑ A system of equations contains two equations and two variables. For example, consider the system of equations: $x - y = 1, x + y = 5$

☑ The easiest way to solve a system of equations is using the elimination method. The elimination method uses the addition property of equality. You can add the same value to each side of an equation.

☑ For the first equation above, you can add $x + y$ to the left side and 5 to the right side of the first equation: $x - y + (x + y) = 1 + 5$. Now, if you simplify, you get: $x - y + (x + y) = 1 + 5 \rightarrow 2x = 6 \rightarrow x = 3$. Now, substitute 3 for the x in the first equation: $3 - y = 1$. By solving this equation, $y = 2$

Example:

What is the value of x + y in this system of equations? $\begin{cases} x + 2y = 6 \\ 2x - y = -8 \end{cases}$

Solution: Solving a System of Equations by Elimination:

Multiply the first equation by (-2), then add it to the second equation.

$$\begin{matrix} -2(x + 2y = 6) \\ 2x - y = -8 \end{matrix} \Rightarrow \begin{matrix} -2x - 4y = -12 \\ 2x - y = -8 \end{matrix} \Rightarrow -5y = -20 \Rightarrow y = 4$$

Plug in the value of y into one of the equations and solve for x.

$x + 2(4) = 6 \Rightarrow x + 8 = 6 \Rightarrow x = 6 - 8 \Rightarrow x = -2$

Thus, $x + y = -2 + 4 = 2$

Graphing Single–Variable Inequalities

☑ An inequality compares two expressions using an inequality sign.

☑ Inequality signs are: "less than" <, "greater than" >, "less than or equal to" ≤, and "greater than or equal to" ≥.

☑ To graph a single-variable inequality, find the value of the inequality on the number line.

☑ For less than (<) or greater than (>) draw open circle on the value of the variable. If there is an equal sign too, then use filled circle.

☑ Draw an arrow to the right for greater or to the left for less than.

Examples:

1) Draw a graph for this inequality. $x > 3$

Solution: Since, the variable is greater than 3, then we need to find 3 in the number line and draw an open circle on it.

Then, draw an arrow to the right.

2) Graph this inequality. $x \leq -4$.

Solution: Since, the variable is less than or equal to -4, then we need to find -4 in the number line and draw a filled circle on it. Then, draw an arrow to the left.

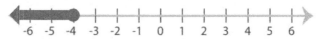

SSAT Middle Level Math Prep 2020-2021

One–Step Inequalities

☑ An inequality compares two expressions using an inequality sign.

☑ Inequality signs are: "less than" <, "greater than" >, "less than or equal to" ≤, and "greater than or equal to" ≥.

☑ You only need to perform one Math operation in order to solve the one-step inequalities.

☑ To solve one-step inequalities, find the inverse (opposite) operation is being performed.

☑ For dividing or multiplying both sides by negative numbers, flip the direction of the inequality sign.

Examples:

1) *Solve this inequality for* x. $x + 3 \geq 4$

Solution: The inverse (opposite) operation of addition is subtraction. In this inequality, 3 is added to x. *To isolate* x *we need to* subtract 3 from both sides of the inequality. Then:

$x + 3 \geq 4 \rightarrow x + 3 - 3 \geq 4 - 3 \rightarrow x \geq 1$. The solution is: $x \geq 1$

2) *Solve the inequality.* $x - 5 > -4$.

Solution: 5 is subtracted from x. Add 5 to both sides. $x - 5 > -4 \rightarrow x - 5 + 5 > -4 + 5 \rightarrow x > 1$

3) *Solve.* $2x \leq -4$.

Solution: 2 is multiplied to x. Divide both sides by 2. Then: $2x \leq -4 \rightarrow \frac{2x}{2} \leq \frac{-4}{2} \rightarrow x \leq -2$

4) *Solve.* $-6x \leq 12$.

Solution: -6 is multiplied to x. Divide both sides by -6. Remember when dividing or multiplying both sides of an inequality by negative numbers, flip the direction of the inequality sign. Then:

$$-6x \leq 12 \rightarrow \frac{-6x}{-6} \geq \frac{12}{-6} \rightarrow x \geq -2$$

Multi–Step Inequalities

☑ To solve a multi-step inequality, combine "like" terms on one side.

☑ Bring variables to one side by adding or subtracting.

☑ Isolate the variable.

☑ Simplify using the inverse of addition or subtraction.

☑ Simplify further by using the inverse of multiplication or division.

☑ For dividing or multiplying both sides by negative numbers, flip the direction of the inequality sign.

Examples:

1) *Solve this inequality.* $2x - 3 \leq 5$

   Solution: In this inequality, 3 is subtracted from $2x$. The inverse of subtraction is addition. Add 3 to both sides of the inequality: $2x - 3 + 3 \leq 5 + 3 \rightarrow 2x \leq 8$

   Now, divide both sides by 2. Then: $2x \leq 8 \rightarrow \frac{2x}{2} \leq \frac{8}{2} \rightarrow x \leq 4$

   The solution of this inequality is $x \leq 4$.

2) *Solve this inequality.* $3x + 9 < 12$

   Solution: First subtract 9 from both sides: $3x + 9 - 9 < 12 - 9$

   Then simplify: $3x + 9 - 9 < 12 - 9 \rightarrow 3x < 3$

   Now divide both sides by 3: $\frac{3x}{3} < \frac{3}{3} \rightarrow x < 1$

3) *Solve this inequality.* $-2x + 4 \geq 6$

   First subtract 4 from both sides: $-2x + 4 - 4 \geq 6 - 4 \rightarrow -2x \geq 2$

   Divide both sides by -2. Remember that you need to flip the direction of inequality sign.

   $$-2x \geq 2 \rightarrow \frac{-2x}{-2} \leq \frac{2}{-2} \rightarrow x \leq -1$$

Chapter 7: Practices

✎ **Solve each equation. (One–Step Equations)**

1) $x + 7 = 6, x = $ ____

2) $8 = 2 - x, x = $ ____

3) $-10 = 8 + x, x = $ ____

4) $x - 5 = -1, x = $ ____

5) $16 = x + 9, x = $ ____

6) $12 - x = -5, x = $ ____

✎ **Solve each equation. (Multi–Step Equations)**

7) $5(x + 3) = 20$

8) $-4(7 - x) = 16$

9) $8 = -2 (x + 5)$

10) $14 = 3(4 - 2x)$

11) $5(x + 7) = -10$

12) $-2(6 + 3x) = 12$

✎ **Solve each system of equations.**

13) $-5x + y = -3$ $x = $
    $3x - 8y = 24$ $y = $

14) $3x - 2y = 2$ $x = $
    $x - y = 2$ $y = $

15) $4x + 7y = 2$ $x = $
    $6x + 7y = 10$ $y = $

16) $5x + 7y = 18$ $x = $
    $-3x + 7y = -22$ $y = $

✎ **Draw a graph for each inequality.**

17) $x \leq -2$

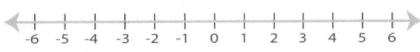

18) $x > -6$

 *Solve each inequality and graph it.*

19) $x - 3 \geq -1$

20) $3x - 2 < 16$

Solve each inequality.

21) $3x + 15 > -6$

22) $-18 + 4x \leq 10$

23) $4(x + 5) \geq 8$

24) $7x - 16 < 12$

25) $3(9 + x) \geq 15$

26) $-8 + 6x > 22$

Answers – Chapter 7

1) -1

2) -6

3) -18

4) 4

5) 7

6) 17

7) 1

8) 11

9) -9

10) $-\frac{1}{3}$

11) -9

12) -4

13) $x = 0$, $y = -3$

14) $x = -2$, $y = -4$

15) $x = 4$, $y = -2$

16) $x = 5$, $y = -1$

17)

18)

19)

20)

21) $x > -7$

22) $x \leq 7$

23) $x \geq -3$

24) $x < 4$

25) $x \geq -4$

26) $x > 5$

Chapter 8:

Exponents and Variables

Math Topics that you'll learn in this Chapter:

- ✓ Multiplication Property of Exponents
- ✓ Division Property of Exponents
- ✓ Powers of Products and Quotients
- ✓ Zero and Negative Exponents
- ✓ Negative Exponents and Negative Bases
- ✓ Scientific Notation
- ✓ Radicals

Multiplication Property of Exponents

☑ Exponents are shorthand for repeated multiplication of the same number by itself. For example, instead of 2×2, we can write 2^2. For $3 \times 3 \times 3 \times 3$, we can write 3^4

☑ In algebra, a variable is a letter used to stand for a number. The most common letters are: x, y, z, a, b, c, m, and n.

☑ Exponent's rules: $x^a \times x^b = x^{a+b}$, $\frac{x^a}{x^b} = x^{a-b}$

$$(x^a)^b = x^{a \times b} \qquad (xy)^a = x^a \times y^a \qquad (\frac{a}{b})^c = \frac{a^c}{b^c}$$

Examples:

1) *Multiply.* $4x^3 \times 2x^2$

   Solution: Use Exponent's rules: $x^a \times x^b = x^{a+b} \rightarrow x^3 \times x^2 = x^{3+2} = x^5$

   Then: $4x^3 \times 2x^2 = 8x^5$

2) *Simplify.* $(x^3 y^5)^2$

   Solution: Use Exponent's rules: $(x^a)^b = x^{a \times b}$. Then: $(x^3 y^5)^2 = x^{3 \times 2} y^{5 \times 2} = x^6 y^{10}$

3) *Multiply.* $-2x^5 \times 7x^3$

   Solution: Use Exponent's rules: $x^a \times x^b = x^{a+b} \rightarrow x^5 \times x^3 = x^{5+3} = x^8$

   Then: $-2x^5 \times 7x^3 = -14x^8$

4) *Simplify.* $(x^2 y^4)^3$

   Solution: Use Exponent's rules: $(x^a)^b = x^{a \times b}$. Then: $(x^2 y^4)^3 = x^{2 \times 3} y^{4 \times 3} = x^6 y^{12}$

Division Property of Exponents

☑ Exponents are shorthand for repeated multiplication of the same number by itself. For example, instead of 3×3, we can write 3^2. For $2 \times 2 \times 2$, we can write 2^3

☑ For division of exponents use following formulas:

$$\frac{x^a}{x^b} = x^{a-b} \, , x \neq 0, \qquad \frac{x^a}{x^b} = \frac{1}{x^{b-a}} \, , x \neq 0, \qquad \frac{1}{x^b} = x^{-b}$$

Examples:

1) *Simplify.* $\frac{12x^2y}{4xy^3} =$

   Solution: First cancel the common factor: $4 \rightarrow \frac{12x^2y}{4xy^3} = \frac{3x^2y}{xy^3}$

   Use Exponent's rules: $\frac{x^a}{x^b} = x^{a-b} \rightarrow \frac{x^2}{x} = x^{2-1} = x$ and $\frac{y}{y^3} = \frac{1}{y^{3-1}} = \frac{1}{y^2}$

   Then: $\frac{12x^2y}{4xy^3} = \frac{3x}{y^2}$

2) *Simplify.* $\frac{18x^6}{2x^3} =$

   Solution: Use Exponent's rules: $\frac{x^a}{x^b} = x^{b-a} \rightarrow \frac{x^6}{x^3} = x^{6-3} = x^3$

   Then: $\frac{18x^6}{2x^3} = 9x^3$

3) *Simplify.* $\frac{8x^3y}{40x^2y^3} =$

   Solution: First cancel the common factor: $8 \rightarrow \frac{8x^3y}{40x^2y^3} = \frac{x^3y}{5x^2y^3}$

   Use Exponent's rules: $\frac{x^a}{x^b} = x^{a-b} \rightarrow \frac{x^3}{x^2} = x^{3-2} = x$

   Then: $\frac{8x^3y}{40x^2y^3} = \frac{xy}{5y^3} \rightarrow$ now cancel the common factor: $y \rightarrow \frac{xy}{5y^3} = \frac{x}{5y^2}$

SSAT Middle Level Math Prep 2020-2021

Powers of Products and Quotients

- ☑ Exponents are shorthand for repeated multiplication of the same number by itself. For example, instead of $2 \times 2 \times 2$, we can write 2^3. For $3 \times 3 \times 3 \times 3$, we can write 3^4

- ☑ For any nonzero numbers a and b and any integer x, $(ab)^x = a^x \times b^x$ and $\left(\frac{a}{b}\right)^c = \frac{a^c}{b^c}$

Examples:

1) *Simplify.* $(6x^2y^4)^2$

   Solution: Use Exponent's rules: $(x^a)^b = x^{a \times b}$

   $(6x^2y^4)^2 = (6)^2(x^2)^2(y^4)^2 = 36x^{2\times2}y^{4\times2} = 36x^4y^8$

2) *Simplify.* $\left(\frac{5x}{2x^2}\right)^2$

   Solution: First cancel the common factor: $x \rightarrow \left(\frac{5x}{2x^2}\right)^2 = \left(\frac{5}{2x}\right)^2$

   Use Exponent's rules: $\left(\frac{a}{b}\right)^c = \frac{a^c}{b^c}$, Then: $\left(\frac{5}{2x}\right)^2 = \frac{5^2}{(2x)^2} = \frac{25}{4x^2}$

3) *Simplify.* $(3x^5y^4)^2$

   Solution: Use Exponent's rules: $(x^a)^b = x^{a \times b}$

   $(3x^5y^4)^2 = (3)^2(x^5)^2(y^4)^2 = 9x^{5\times2}y^{4\times2} = 9x^{10}y^8$

4) *Simplify.* $\left(\frac{2x}{3x^2}\right)^2$

   Solution: First cancel the common factor: $x \rightarrow \left(\frac{2x}{3x^2}\right)^2 = \left(\frac{2}{3x}\right)^2$

   Use Exponent's rules: $\left(\frac{a}{b}\right)^c = \frac{a^c}{b^c}$, Then: $\left(\frac{2}{3x}\right)^2 = \frac{2^2}{(3x)^2} = \frac{4}{9x^2}$

Zero and Negative Exponents

☑ Zero-Exponent Rule: $a^0 = 1$, this means that anything raised to the zero power is 1. For example: $(5xy)^0 = 1$

☑ A negative exponent simply means that the base is on the wrong side of the fraction line, so you need to flip the base to the other side. For instance, "x^{-2}" (pronounced as "ecks to the minus two") just means "x^2" but underneath, as in $\frac{1}{x^2}$.

Examples:

1) Evaluate. $\left(\frac{2}{3}\right)^{-2} =$

Solution: Use negative exponent's rule: $\left(\frac{x^a}{x^b}\right)^{-2} = \left(\frac{x^b}{x^a}\right)^2 \rightarrow \left(\frac{2}{3}\right)^{-2} = \left(\frac{3}{2}\right)^2 =$
Then: $\left(\frac{3}{2}\right)^2 = \frac{3^2}{2^2} = \frac{9}{4}$

2) Evaluate. $\left(\frac{4}{5}\right)^{-3} =$

Solution: Use negative exponent's rule: $\left(\frac{x^a}{x^b}\right)^{-2} = \left(\frac{x^b}{x^a}\right)^2 \rightarrow \left(\frac{4}{5}\right)^{-3} = \left(\frac{5}{4}\right)^3 =$
Then: $\left(\frac{5}{4}\right)^3 = \frac{5^3}{4^3} = \frac{125}{64}$

3) Evaluate. $\left(\frac{x}{y}\right)^0 =$

Solution: Use zero-exponent Rule: $a^0 = 1$
Then: $\left(\frac{x}{y}\right)^0 = 1$

4) Evaluate. $\left(\frac{5}{6}\right)^{-1} =$

Solution: Use negative exponent's rule: $\left(\frac{x^a}{x^b}\right)^{-2} = \left(\frac{x^b}{x^a}\right)^2 \rightarrow \left(\frac{5}{6}\right)^{-1} = \left(\frac{6}{5}\right)^1 = \frac{6}{5}$

Negative Exponents and Negative Bases

☑ A negative exponent is the reciprocal of that number with a positive exponent. $(3)^{-2} = \frac{1}{3^2}$

☑ To simplify a negative exponent, make the power positive!

☑ The parenthesis is important! -5^{-2} is not the same as $(-5)^{-2}$

$$-5^{-2} = -\frac{1}{5^2} \text{ and } (-5)^{-2} = +\frac{1}{5^2}$$

Examples:

1) *Simplify.* $(\frac{5a}{6c})^{-2} =$

   Solution: Use negative exponent's rule: $(\frac{x^a}{x^b})^{-2} = (\frac{x^b}{x^a})^2 \rightarrow (\frac{5a}{6c})^{-2} = (\frac{6c}{5a})^2$

   Now use exponent's rule: $(\frac{a}{b})^c = \frac{a^c}{b^c} \rightarrow = (\frac{6c}{5a})^2 = \frac{6^2 c^2}{5^2 a^2}$

   Then: $\frac{6^2 c^2}{5^2 a^2} = \frac{36c^2}{25a^2}$

2) *Simplify.* $(\frac{2x}{3yz})^{-3} =$

   Solution: Use negative exponent's rule: $(\frac{x^a}{x^b})^{-2} = (\frac{x^b}{x^a})^2 \rightarrow (\frac{2x}{3yz})^{-3} = (\frac{3yz}{2x})^3$

   Now use exponent's rule: $(\frac{a}{b})^c = \frac{a^c}{b^c} \rightarrow (\frac{3yz}{2x})^3 = \frac{3^3 y^3 z^3}{2^3 x^3} = \frac{27y^3 z^3}{8x^3}$

3) *Simplify.* $(\frac{3a}{2c})^{-2} =$

   Solution: Use negative exponent's rule: $(\frac{x^a}{x^b})^{-2} = (\frac{x^b}{x^a})^2 \rightarrow (\frac{3a}{2c})^{-2} = (\frac{2c}{3a})^2$

   Now use exponent's rule: $(\frac{a}{b})^c = \frac{a^c}{b^c} \rightarrow = (\frac{2c}{3a})^2 = \frac{2^2 c^2}{3^2 a^2}$

   Then: $\frac{2^2 c^2}{3^2 a^2} = \frac{4c^2}{9a^2}$

Scientific Notation

☑ Scientific notation is used to write very big or very small numbers in decimal form.

☑ In scientific notation all numbers are written in the form of: $m \times 10^n$, where m is greater than 1 and less than 10.

☑ To convert a number from scientific notation to standard form, move the decimal point to the left (if the exponent of ten is a negative number), or to the right (if the exponent is positive).

Examples:

1) *Write 0.00015 in scientific notation.*

   Solution: First, move the decimal point to the right so that you have a number that is between 1 and 10. That number is 1.5
   Now, determine how many places the decimal moved in step 1 by the power of 10. We moved the decimal point 4 digits to the right. Then: $10^{-4} \rightarrow$ When the decimal moved to the right, the exponent is negative. Then: $0.00015 = 1.5 \times 10^{-4}$

2) *Write 9.5×10^{-5} in standard notation.*

   Solution: $10^{-5} \rightarrow$ When the decimal moved to the right, the exponent is negative.
   Then: $9.5 \times 10^{-5} = 0.000095$

3) *Write 0.00012 in scientific notation.*

   Solution: First, move the decimal point to the right so that you have a number that is between 1 and 10. Then: $m = 1.2$
   Now, determine how many places the decimal moved in step 1 by the power of 10.
   $10^{-4} \rightarrow$ Then: $0.00012 = 1.2 \times 10^{-4}$

4) *Write 8.3×10^5 in standard notation.*

   Solution: $10^{-5} \rightarrow$ The exponent is positive 5. Then, move the decimal point to the right five digits. (remember $8.3 = 8.30000$)
   Then: $8.3 \times 10^5 = 830000$

Radicals

☑ If n is a positive integer and x is a real number, then: $\sqrt[n]{x} = x^{\frac{1}{n}}$,
$\sqrt[n]{xy} = x^{\frac{1}{n}} \times y^{\frac{1}{n}}$, $\sqrt[n]{\frac{x}{y}} = \frac{x^{\frac{1}{n}}}{y^{\frac{1}{n}}}$, and $\sqrt[n]{x} \times \sqrt[n]{y} = \sqrt[n]{xy}$

☑ A square root of x is a number r whose square is: $r^2 = x$ (r is a square root of x.

☑ To add and subtract radicals, we need to have the same values under the radical. For example: $\sqrt{3} + \sqrt{3} = 2\sqrt{3}$, $3\sqrt{5} - \sqrt{5} = 2\sqrt{5}$

Examples:

1) *Find the square root of* $\sqrt{169}$.

   Solution: First factor the number: $169 = 13^2$,

   Then: $\sqrt{169} = \sqrt{13^2}$

   Now use radical rule: $\sqrt[n]{a^n} = a$.

   Then: $\sqrt{169} = \sqrt{13^2} = 13$

2) *Evaluate.* $\sqrt{9} \times \sqrt{25} =$

   Solution: Find the values of $\sqrt{9}$ and $\sqrt{25}$.

   Then: $\sqrt{9} \times \sqrt{25} = 3 \times 5 = 15$

3) *Solve.* $7\sqrt{2} + 4\sqrt{2}$.

   Solution: Since we have the same values under the radical, we can add these two radicals:
   $7\sqrt{2} + 4\sqrt{2} = 11\sqrt{2}$

4) *Evaluate.* $\sqrt{2} \times \sqrt{8} =$

   Solution: Use this radical rule: $\sqrt[n]{x} \times \sqrt[n]{y} = \sqrt[n]{xy} \rightarrow \sqrt{2} \times \sqrt{8} = \sqrt{16}$

   The square root of 16 is 4. Then: $\sqrt{2} \times \sqrt{8} = \sqrt{16} = 4$

Chapter 8: Practices

✐ *Simplify and write the answer in exponential form.*

1) $3x^3 \times 5xy^2 =$

2) $4x^2y \times 6x^2y^2 =$

3) $8x^3y^2 \times 2x^2y^3 =$

4) $7xy^4 \times 3x^2y =$

5) $6x^4y^5 \times 8x^3y^2 =$

6) $5x^3y^3 \times 8x^3y^3 =$

✐ *Simplify. (Division Property of Exponents)*

7) $\dfrac{5^5 \times 5^3}{5^9 \times 5} =$

8) $\dfrac{8x}{24^2} =$

9) $\dfrac{15x^4}{9x^3} =$

10) $\dfrac{36^3}{54x^3y^2} =$

11) $\dfrac{14^3}{49^4y^4} =$

12) $\dfrac{120x^3y^5}{30^2y^3} =$

✐ *Simplify. (Powers of Products and Quotients)*

13) $(8x^4y^6)^3 =$

14) $(3x^5y^4)^6 =$

15) $(5x \times 4xy^2)^2 =$

16) $\left(\dfrac{6x}{x^3}\right)^2 =$

17) $\left(\dfrac{2x^3y^5}{6x^4y^2}\right)^2 =$

18) $\left(\dfrac{42x^4y^6}{21^3y^5}\right)^3 =$

✐ *Evaluate the following expressions. (Zero and Negative Exponents)*

19) $\left(\dfrac{2}{5}\right)^{-2} =$

20) $\left(\dfrac{1}{2}\right)^{-8} =$

21) $\left(\dfrac{2}{5}\right)^{-3} =$

22) $\left(\dfrac{3}{7}\right)^{-2} =$

23) $\left(\dfrac{5}{6}\right)^{-3} =$

24) $\left(\dfrac{4}{9}\right)^{-2} =$

✐ *Simplify. (Negative Exponents and Negative Bases)*

25) $16x^{-3}y^{-4} =$

26) $-9x^2y^{-3} =$

27) $12a^{-4}b^2 =$

28) $25a^3b^{-5}c^{-1} =$

29) $\dfrac{18}{x^2y^{-2}} =$

30) $\dfrac{21^{-2}b}{-14c^{-4}} =$

✍ *Write each number in scientific notation.*

31) $0.00615 =$

32) $0.000048 =$

33) $36,000 =$

34) $82,000,000 =$

✍ *Evaluate.*

35) $\sqrt{7} \times \sqrt{7} =$ _____

36) $\sqrt{36} - \sqrt{9} =$ _____

37) $\sqrt{25} + \sqrt{49} =$ _____

38) $\sqrt{16} \times \sqrt{64} =$ _____

39) $\sqrt{3} \times \sqrt{12} =$ _____

40) $2\sqrt{6} + 3\sqrt{6} =$ _____

Answers – Chapter 8

1) $15x^4y^2$

2) $24x^4y^3$

3) $16x^5y^5$

4) $21x^3y^5$

5) $48x^7y^7$

6) $40x^6y^6$

7) $\frac{1}{25}$

8) $\frac{1}{3x}$

9) $\frac{5}{3}x$

10) $\frac{2}{3y^3}$

11) $\frac{2}{7x^4y}$

12) $4xy^2$

13) $512x^{12}y^{18}$

14) $729x^{30}y^{24}$

15) $400x^4y^4$

16) $\frac{36}{x^4}$

17) $\frac{y^6}{9x^2}$

18) $8x^3y^3$

19) $\frac{25}{4}$

20) 256

21) $\frac{125}{8}$

22) $\frac{49}{9}$

23) $\frac{216}{125}$

24) $\frac{81}{16}$

25) $\frac{16}{x^3y^4}$

26) $-\frac{9x^2}{y^3}$

27) $\frac{12b^2}{a^4}$

28) $\frac{25a^3}{b^5c}$

29) $\frac{18\ ^3}{x^2}$

30) $-\frac{3bc^4}{2a^2}$

31) 6.15×10^{-3}

32) 4.8×10^{-5}

33) 3.6×10^4

34) 8.2×10^7

35) 7

36) 3

37) 12

38) 32

39) 6

40) $5\sqrt{6}$

Chapter 9:

Geometry and Solid Figures

Math Topics that you'll learn in this Chapter:

- ✓ The Pythagorean Theorem
- ✓ Triangles
- ✓ Polygons
- ✓ Circles
- ✓ Trapezoids
- ✓ Cubes
- ✓ Rectangle Prisms
- ✓ Cylinder

The Pythagorean Theorem

☑ You can use the Pythagorean Theorem to find a missing side in a right triangle.

☑ In any right triangle: $a^2 + b^2 = c^2$

Examples:

1) Right triangle ABC (not shown) has two legs of lengths 6 cm (AB) and 8 cm (AC). What is the length of the hypotenuse of the triangle (side BC)?

   Solution: Use Pythagorean Theorem: $a^2 + b^2 = c^2$, $a = 6$, and $b = 8$

   Then: $a^2 + b^2 = c^2 \rightarrow 6^2 + 8^2 = c^2 \rightarrow 36 + 64 = c^2 \rightarrow 100 = c^2 \rightarrow c = \sqrt{100} = 10$

   The length of the hypotenuse is 10 cm.

2) Find the hypotenuse of the following triangle.

   Solution: Use Pythagorean Theorem: $a^2 + b^2 = c^2$

   Then: $a^2 + b^2 = c^2 \rightarrow 12^2 + 5^2 = c^2 \rightarrow 144 + 25 = c^2$

   $c^2 = 169 \rightarrow c = \sqrt{169} = 13$

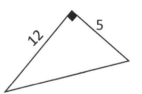

3) Find the length of the missing side in the following triangle.

   Solution: Use Pythagorean Theorem: $a^2 + b^2 = c^2$

   Then: $a^2 + b^2 = c^2 \rightarrow 3^2 + b^2 = 5^2 \rightarrow 9 + b^2 = 25 \rightarrow$

   $b^2 = 25 - 9 \rightarrow b^2 = 16 \rightarrow b = \sqrt{16} = 4$

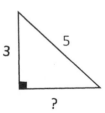

Triangles

☑ In any triangle the sum of all angles is 180 degrees.

☑ Area of a triangle $= \frac{1}{2}\,(base \times height)$

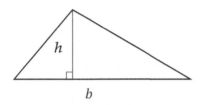

Examples:

What is the area of following triangles?

1)

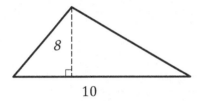

Solution:
Use the area formula: Area $= \frac{1}{2}\,(base \times height)$
$base = 10$ and $height = 8$
Area $= \frac{1}{2}(10 \times 8) = \frac{1}{2}(80) = 40$

2)

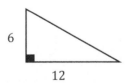

Solution:
Use the area formula: Area $= \frac{1}{2}\,(base \times height)$
$base = 12$ and $height = 6$
Area $= \frac{1}{2}(12 \times 6) = \frac{72}{2} = 36$

3) What is the missing angle in the following triangle?

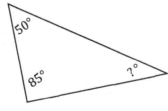

Solution:
In any triangle the sum of all angles is 180 degrees.
Let x be the missing angle. Then: $50 + 85 + x = 180$
    $\rightarrow 135 + x = 180 \rightarrow x = 180 - 135 = 45$
The missing angle is 45 degrees.

Polygons

☑ **Perimeter of a square**

$= 4 \times side = 4s$

☑ **Perimeter of a rectangle**

$= 2(width + length)$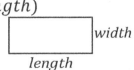

☑ **Perimeter of trapezoid**

$= a + b + c + d$

☑ **Perimeter of a regular hexagon** $= 6a$

☑ **Perimeter of a parallelogram** $= 2(l + w)$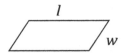

Examples:

1) Find the perimeter of following regular hexagon.

   Solution: Since the hexagon is regular, all sides are equal.

   Then: Perimeter of Hexagon $= 6 \times (one\ side)$

   Perimeter of Hexagon $= 6 \times (one\ side) = 6 \times 4 = 24\ m$

2) Find the perimeter of following trapezoid.

   Solution: Perimeter of a trapezoid $= a + b + c + d$

   Perimeter of the trapezoid $= 5 + 6 + 6 + 8 = 25\ ft$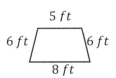

SSAT Middle Level Math Prep 2020-2021

Circles

☑ In a circle, variable r is usually used for the radius and d for diameter.

☑ *Area of a circle* $= \pi r^2$ (π is about 3.14)

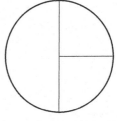

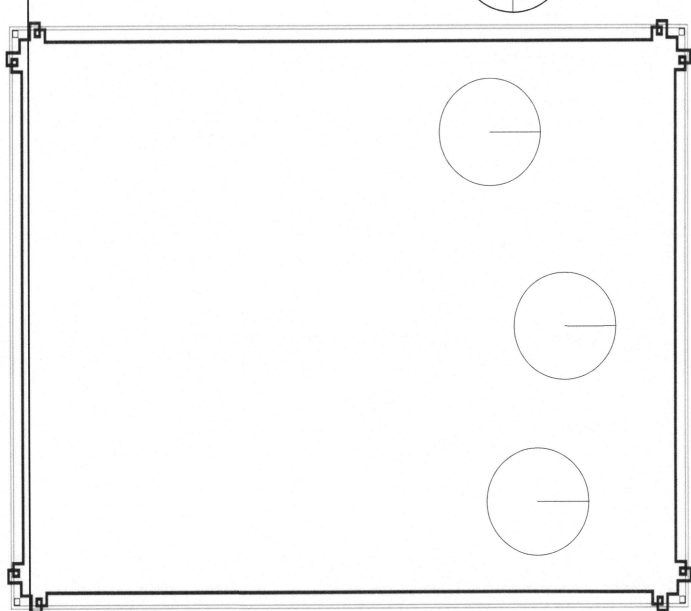

Trapezoids

☑ A quadrilateral with at least one pair of parallel sides is a trapezoid.

☑ Area of a trapezoid $= \frac{1}{2}h(b_1 + b_2)$

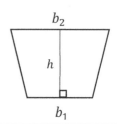

Examples:

1) Calculate the area of the following trapezoid.

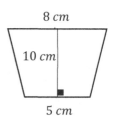

Solution:

Use area formula: $A = \frac{1}{2}h(b_1 + b_2)$

$b_1 = 5\ cm$, $b_2 = 8\ cm$ and $h = 10\ cm$

Then: $A = \frac{1}{2}(10)(8 + 5) = 5(13) = 65\ cm^2$

2) Calculate the area of the following trapezoid.

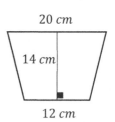

Solution:

Use area formula: $A = \frac{1}{2}h(b_1 + b_2)$

$b_1 = 12\ cm$, $b_2 = 20\ cm$ and $h = 14\ cm$

Then: $A = \frac{1}{2}(14)(12 + 20) = 7(32) = 224\ cm^2$

SSAT Middle Level Math Prep 2020-2021

Cubes

☑ A cube is a three-dimensional solid object bounded by six square sides.

☑ Volume is the measure of the amount of space inside of a solid figure, like a cube, ball, cylinder or pyramid.

☑ Volume of a cube = $(one\ side)^3$

☑ surface area of a cube = $6 \times (one\ side)^2$

Examples:

1) Find the volume and surface area of the following cube.

   Solution: Use volume formula: $volume = (one\ side)^3$

   Then: $volume = (one\ side)^3 = (2)^3 = 8\ cm^3$

   Use surface area formula: $surface\ area\ of\ cube: 6(one\ side)^2 =$
   $$6(2)^2 = 6(4) = 24\ cm^2$$

2 cm

2) Find the volume and surface area of the following cube.

   Solution: Use volume formula: $volume = (one\ side)^3$

   Then: $volume = (one\ side)^3 = (5)^3 = 125\ cm^3$

   Use surface area formula:

   $surface\ area\ of\ cube: 6(one\ side)^2 = 6(5)^2 = 6(25) = 150\ cm^2$

5 cm

3) Find the volume and surface area of the following cube.

   Solution: Use volume formula: $volume = (one\ side)^3$

   Then: $volume = (one\ side)^3 = (7)^3 = 343\ m^3$

   Use surface area formula:

   $surface\ area\ of\ cube: 6(one\ side)^2 = 6(7)^2 = 6(49) = 294\ m^2$

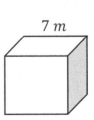
7 m

Rectangular Prisms

☑ A rectangular prism is a solid 3-dimensional object which has six rectangular faces.

☑ Volume of a Rectangular prism = **$Length \times Width \times Height$**

$Volume = l \times w \times h$

$Surface\ area = 2 \times (wh + lw + lh)$

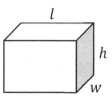

Examples:

1) Find the volume and surface area of the following rectangular prism.

   Solution:

   Use volume formula: $Volume = l \times w \times h$

   Then: $Volume = 8 \times 6 \times 10 = 480\ m^3$

   Use surface area formula: $Surface\ area = 2 \times (wh + lw + lh)$

   Then: $Surface\ area = 2 \times \big((6 \times 10) + (8 \times 6) + (8 \times 10)\big)$

   $= 2 \times (60 + 48 + 80) = 2 \times (188) = 376\ m^2$

2) Find the volume and surface area of rectangular prism.

   Solution:

   Use volume formula: $Volume = l \times w \times h$

   Then: $Volume = 10 \times 8 \times 12 = 960\ m^3$

   Use surface area formula: $Surface\ area = 2 \times (wh + lw + lh)$

   Then: $Surface\ area = 2 \times \big((8 \times 12) + (10 \times 8) + (10 \times 12)\big)$

   $= 2 \times (96 + 80 + 120) = 2 \times (296) = 592\ m^2$

Cylinder

☑ A cylinder is a solid geometric figure with straight parallel sides and a circular or oval cross section.

☑ *Volume of a Cylinder* $= \pi(radius)^2 \times height$, $\pi \approx 3.14$

☑ *Surface area of a cylinder* $= 2\pi r^2 + 2\pi rh$

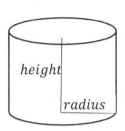

Examples:

1) *Find the volume and Surface area of the follow Cylinder.*

Solution:

Use volume formula: $Volume = \pi(radius)^2 \times height$
Then: $Volume = \pi(3)^2 \times 8 = 9\pi \times 8 = 72\pi$
$\pi = 3.14$ **then:** $Volume = 72\pi = 72 \times 3.14 = 226.08 \ cm^3$
Use surface area formula: $Surface \ area = 2\pi r^2 + 2\pi rh$
Then: $2\pi(3)^2 + 2\pi(3)(8) = 2\pi(9) + 2\pi(24) = 18\pi + 48\pi = 66\pi$
$\pi = 3.14$ Then: $Surface \ area = 66 \times 3.14 = 207.24 \ cm^2$

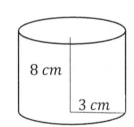

2) *Find the volume and Surface area of the follow Cylinder.*

Solution:

Use volume formula: $Volume = \pi(radius)^2 \times height$
Then: $Volume = \pi(2)^2 \times 6 = \pi 4 \times 6 = 24\pi$
$\pi = 3.14$ **then:** $Volume = 24\pi = 75.36 \ cm^3$
Use surface area formula: $Surface \ area = 2\pi r^2 + 2\pi rh$
Then: $= 2\pi(2)^2 + 2\pi(2)(6) = 2\pi(4) + 2\pi(12) = 8\pi + 24\pi = 32\pi$
$\pi = 3.14$ **then:** $Surface \ area = 32 \times 3.14 = 100.48 \ cm^2$

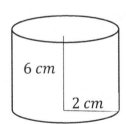

Chapter 9: Practices

✎ *Find the missing side?*

1)

5
3
?

2)
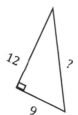
12
?
9

3)
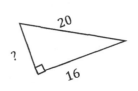
20
?
16

4)
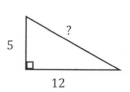
?
5
12

✎ *Find the measure of the unknown angle in each triangle.*

5)
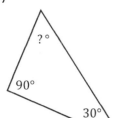
?°
90°
30°

6)
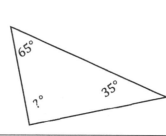
65°
?°
35°

7)
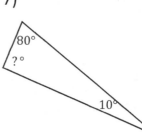
80°
?°
10°

8)
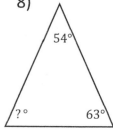
54°
?°
63°

✎ *Find area of each triangle.*

9)
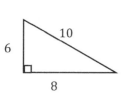
10
6
8

10)
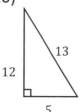
13
12
5

11)
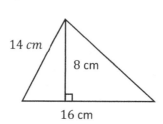
14 cm
8 cm
16 cm

12)
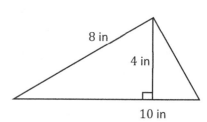
8 in
4 in
10 in

✎ *Find the perimeter of each shape.*

13)
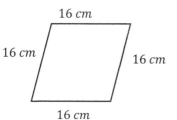
16 cm
16 cm
16 cm
16 cm

14)
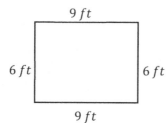
9 ft
6 ft
6 ft
9 ft

15)
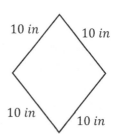
10 in
10 in
10 in
10 in

16)
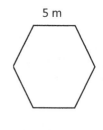
5 m

🖊 **Complete the table below.** (π = 3.14)

17)

	Radius	Diameter	Circumference	Area
Circle 1	3 inches	6 inches	18.84 inches	28.26 square inches
Circle 2			43.96 meters	
Circle 3		8 ft		
Circle 4				78.5 square miles

🖊 **Find the area of each trapezoid.**

18)
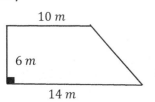

10 m

6 m

14 m

19)
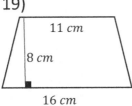

11 cm

8 cm

16 cm

20)
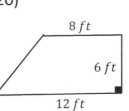

8 ft

6 ft

12 ft

21)
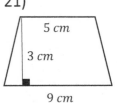

5 cm

3 cm

9 cm

🖊 **Find the volume of each cube.**

22)
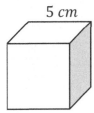

5 cm

23)
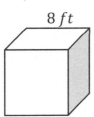

8 ft

24)
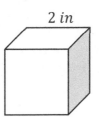

2 in

25)
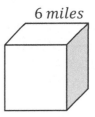

6 miles

🖊 **Find the volume of each Rectangular Prism.**

26)
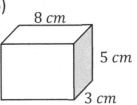

8 cm

5 cm

3 cm

27)
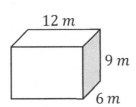

12 m

9 m

6 m

28)
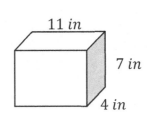

11 in

7 in

4 in

Find the volume of each Cylinder. Round your answer to the nearest tenth. ($\pi = 3.14$)

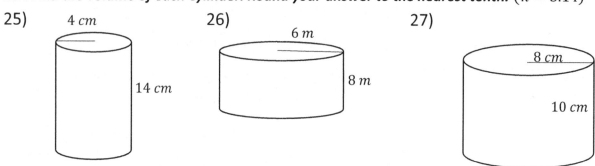

25) 4 cm, 14 cm

26) 6 m, 8 m

27) 8 cm, 10 cm

Answers – Chapter 9

1) 4

2) 15

3) 12

4) 13

5) 60°

6) 80°

7) 90°

8) 63°

9) 24 *square unites*

10) 30 *square unites*

11) 64 cm^2

12) 20 in^2

13) 64 *cm*

14) 30 *ft*

15) 40 *in*

16) 30 *m*

17)

	Radius	Diameter	Circumference	Area
Circle 1	3 *inches*	6 *inches*	18.84 *inches*	28.26 *square inches*
Circle 2	7 *meters*	14 *meters*	43.96 *meters*	153.86 *square meters*
Circle 3	4 *ft*	8 *ft*	25.12 *ft*	50.24 *square ft*
Circle 4	5 *miles*	10 *miles*	31.4 *miles*	78.5 *square miles*

18) 72 m^2

19) 108 cm^2

20) 60 ft^2

21) 21 cm^2

22) 125 cm^3

23) 512 ft^3

24) 8 in^3

25) 216 $miles^3$

26) 120 cm^3

27) 648 m^3

28) 308 in^3

29) 703.36 cm^3

30) 904.32 m^3

31) 2,009.6 cm^3

Chapter 10:

Statistics

Math Topics that you'll learn in this Chapter:

- ✓ Mean, Median, Mode, and Range of the Given Data

- ✓ Pie Graph

- ✓ Probability Problems

- ✓ Permutations and Combinations

Mean, Median, Mode, and Range of the Given Data

☑ Mean: $\dfrac{sum\ of\ the\ data}{total\ number\ of\ data\ entires}$

☑ Mode: the value in the list that appears most often

☑ Median: is the middle number of a group of numbers that have been arranged in order by size.

☑ Range: the difference of largest value and smallest value in the list

Examples:

1) What is the mode of these numbers? $4, 5, 7, 5, 7, 4, 0, 4$

   Solution: Mode: the value in the list that appears most often.
   Therefore, the mode is number 4. There are three number 4 in the data.

2) What is the median of these numbers? $5, 10, 14, 9, 16, 19, 6$

   Solution: Write the numbers in order: $5, 6, 9, 10, 14, 16, 19$

   Median is the number in the middle. Therefore, the median is 10.

3) What is the mean of these numbers? $8, 2, 8, 5, 3, 2, 4, 8$

   Solution: Mean: $\dfrac{sum\ of\ the\ data}{total\ number\ of\ data\ entires} = \dfrac{8+2+8+5+3+2+4+8}{8} = 5$

4) What is the range in this list? $4, 9, 13, 8, 15, 18, 5$

   Solution: Range is the difference of largest value and smallest value in the list. The largest value is 18 and the smallest value is 4. Then: $18 - 4 = 14$

Pie Graph

☑ A Pie Chart is a circle chart divided into sectors, each sector represents the relative size of each value.

☑ Pie charts represent a snapshot of how a group is broken down into smaller pieces.

Example:

A library has 820 books that include Mathematics, Physics, Chemistry, English and History. Use following graph to answer the questions.

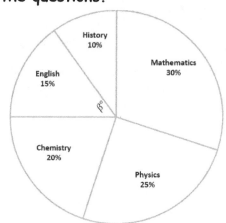

1) What is the number of Mathematics books?

   Solution: Number of total books = 820

   Percent of Mathematics books = 30% = 0.30

   Then, number of Mathematics books:
   $$0.30 \times 820 = 246$$

2) What is the number of History books?

   Solution: Number of total books = 820

   Percent of History books = 10% = 0.10

   Then: $0.10 \times 820 = 82$

3) What is the number of Chemistry books?

   Solution: Number of total books = 820

   Percent of Chemistry books = 20% = 0.20

   Then: $0.20 \times 820 = 164$

Probability Problems

☑ Probability is the likelihood of something happening in the future. It is expressed as a number between zero (can never happen) to 1 (will always happen).

☑ Probability can be expressed as a fraction, a decimal, or a percent.

☑ Probability formula: $Probability = \frac{number\ of\ desired\ outcomes}{number\ of\ total\ outcomes}$

Examples:

1) Anita's trick-or-treat bag contains 12 pieces of chocolate, 18 suckers, 18 pieces of gum, 24 pieces of licorice. If she randomly pulls a piece of candy from her bag, what is the probability of her pulling out a piece of sucker?

   Solution: $Probability = \frac{number\ of\ desired\ outcomes}{number\ of\ total\ outcomes}$

   Probability of ulling out a piece of sucker $= \frac{18}{12 + 18 + 18 + 24} = \frac{18}{72} = \frac{1}{4}$

2) A bag contains 20 balls: four green, five black, eight blue, a brown, a red and one white. If 19 balls are removed from the bag at random, what is the probability that a brown ball has been removed?

   Solution: If 19 balls are removed from the bag at random, there will be one ball in the bag. The probability of choosing a brown ball is 1 out of 20. Therefore, the probability of not choosing a brown ball is 19 out of 20 and the probability of having not a brown ball after removing 19 balls is the same.

Permutations and Combinations

☑ Factorials are products, indicated by an exclamation mark. For example, $4! = 4 \times 3 \times 2 \times 1$ (Remember that $0!$ is defined to be equal to 1.)

☑ Permutations: The number of ways to choose a sample of k elements from a set of n distinct objects where order does matter, and replacements are not allowed. For a permutation problem, use this formula:

$$_nP_k = \frac{n!}{(n-k)!}$$

☑ Combination: The number of ways to choose a sample of r elements from a set of n distinct objects where order does not matter, and replacements are not allowed. For a combination problem, use this formula:

$$_nC_r = \frac{n!}{r!\,(n-r)!}$$

Examples:

1) *How many ways can the first and second place be awarded to 8 people?*

   Solution: Since the order matters, (the first and second place are different!) we need to use permutation formula where n is 10 and k is 2. Then: $\frac{n!}{(n-k)!} = \frac{8!}{(8-2)!} = \frac{8!}{6!} = \frac{8 \times 7 \times 6!}{6!}$, remove 6! from both sides of the fraction. Then: $\frac{8 \times 7 \times 6!}{6!} = 8 \times 7 = 56$

2) *How many ways can we pick a team of 2 people from a group of 6?*

   Solution: Since the order doesn't matter, we need to use combination formula where n is 8 and r is 3. Then: $\frac{n!}{r!\,(n-r)!} = \frac{6!}{2!\,(6-2)!} = \frac{6!}{2!\,(4)!} = \frac{6 \times 5 \times 4!}{2!\,(4)!} = \frac{6 \times 5}{2 \times 1} = \frac{30}{2} = 15$

SSAT Middle Level Math Prep 2020-2021

Chapter 10: Practices

✍ *Find the values of the Given Data.*

1) 6, 12, 1, 1, 5

    Mode: _____   Range: _____

    Mean: _____   Median: _____

2) 5, 8, 3, 7, 4, 3

    Mode: _____   Range: _____

    Mean: _____   Median: _____

✍ The circle graph below shows all Jason's expenses for last month. Jason spent $864 on his bills last month.

3) How much did Jason spend on his car last month? _____

4) How much did Jason spend for foods last month? _____

Jason's last month expenses

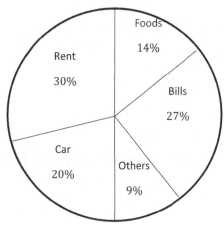

✎ *Solve.*

5) Bag A contains 8 red marbles and 6 green marbles. Bag B contains 5 black marbles and 10 orange marbles. What is the probability of selecting a green marble at random from bag A? What is the probability of selecting a black marble at random from Bag B? _____   _____

✎ *Solve.*

6) Susan is baking cookies. She uses sugar, flour, butter, and eggs. How many different orders of ingredients can she try? _____

7) Jason is planning for his vacation. He wants to go to museum, watch a movie, go to the beach, and play volleyball. How many different ways of ordering are there for him? _____

8) In how many ways a team of 10 basketball players can to choose a captain and co-captain? _____

9) How many ways can you give 3 balls to your 8 friends? _____

10) A professor is going to arrange her 8 students in a straight line. In how many ways can she do this? _____

Answers – Chapter 10

1) Mode: 1 , Range: 11, Mean: 5, Median: 5

2) Mode: 3 , Range: 5 , Mean: 5, Median: 4.5

3) $640

4) $448

5) $\frac{3}{7}, \frac{1}{3}$

6) 24

7) 24

8) 90

9) 56

10) 40,320

SSAT Middle Level Test Review

The SSAT, or Secondary School Admissions Test, is a standardized test to help determine admission to private elementary, middle and high schools.

There are currently three Levels of the SSAT:

- ✓ Lower Level (for students in 3rd and 4th grade)
- ✓ Middle Level (for students in 5th-7th grade)
- ✓ Upper Level (for students in 8th-11th grade)

There are six sections on the SSAT Middle Level Test:

- ✓ Writing: 25 minutes.
- ✓ Math section: 25 questions, 30 minutes
- ✓ Reading section: 40 questions, 40 minutes
- ✓ Verbal section: 60 questions, 30 minutes
- ✓ Math section: 25 questions, 30 minutes
- ✓ Experimental: 16 questions, 15 minutes.

In this book, there are 2 complete SSAT Middle Level Math Practice Tests. Take these tests to see what score you'll be able to receive on a real SSAT Middle Level test.

Good luck!

Time to Test

Time to refine your skill with a practice examination

Take a practice SSAT Middle Level Mathematics Test to simulate the test day experience. After you've finished, score your test using the answer keys.

Before You Start

- You'll need a pencil and a timer to take the test.

- After you've finished the test, review the answer key to see where you went wrong.

- Use the answer sheet provided to record your answers. (You can cut it out or photocopy it)

- You will receive 1 point for every correct answer, and you will lose $\frac{1}{4}$ point for each incorrect answer. There is no penalty for skipping a question.

Calculators are NOT permitted for the SSAT Middle Level Test

Good Luck!

SSAT Middle Level Math

Practice Test 1

2020 - 2021

Two Parts

Total number of questions: 50

Section 1: 25 questions

Section 2: 25 questions

Total time for two parts: 60 Minutes

SSAT Middle Level Math Practice Test 1 Answer Sheet

Remove (or photocopy) this answer sheet and use it to complete the practice test.

SSAT Middle Level Mathematics Practice Test 1 Answer Sheet

SSAT Middle Level Practice Test 1 Section 1

1	Ⓐ Ⓑ Ⓒ Ⓓ Ⓔ	11	Ⓐ Ⓑ Ⓒ Ⓓ Ⓔ	21	Ⓐ Ⓑ Ⓒ Ⓓ Ⓔ
2	Ⓐ Ⓑ Ⓒ Ⓓ Ⓔ	12	Ⓐ Ⓑ Ⓒ Ⓓ Ⓔ	22	Ⓐ Ⓑ Ⓒ Ⓓ Ⓔ
3	Ⓐ Ⓑ Ⓒ Ⓓ Ⓔ	13	Ⓐ Ⓑ Ⓒ Ⓓ Ⓔ	23	Ⓐ Ⓑ Ⓒ Ⓓ Ⓔ
4	Ⓐ Ⓑ Ⓒ Ⓓ Ⓔ	14	Ⓐ Ⓑ Ⓒ Ⓓ Ⓔ	24	Ⓐ Ⓑ Ⓒ Ⓓ Ⓔ
5	Ⓐ Ⓑ Ⓒ Ⓓ Ⓔ	15	Ⓐ Ⓑ Ⓒ Ⓓ Ⓔ	25	Ⓐ Ⓑ Ⓒ Ⓓ Ⓔ
6	Ⓐ Ⓑ Ⓒ Ⓓ Ⓔ	16	Ⓐ Ⓑ Ⓒ Ⓓ Ⓔ		
7	Ⓐ Ⓑ Ⓒ Ⓓ Ⓔ	17	Ⓐ Ⓑ Ⓒ Ⓓ Ⓔ		
8	Ⓐ Ⓑ Ⓒ Ⓓ Ⓔ	18	Ⓐ Ⓑ Ⓒ Ⓓ Ⓔ		
9	Ⓐ Ⓑ Ⓒ Ⓓ Ⓔ	19	Ⓐ Ⓑ Ⓒ Ⓓ Ⓔ		
10	Ⓐ Ⓑ Ⓒ Ⓓ Ⓔ	20	Ⓐ Ⓑ Ⓒ Ⓓ Ⓔ		

SSAT Middle Level Practice Test 1 Section 2

1	Ⓐ Ⓑ Ⓒ Ⓓ Ⓔ	11	Ⓐ Ⓑ Ⓒ Ⓓ Ⓔ	21	Ⓐ Ⓑ Ⓒ Ⓓ Ⓔ
2	Ⓐ Ⓑ Ⓒ Ⓓ Ⓔ	12	Ⓐ Ⓑ Ⓒ Ⓓ Ⓔ	22	Ⓐ Ⓑ Ⓒ Ⓓ Ⓔ
3	Ⓐ Ⓑ Ⓒ Ⓓ Ⓔ	13	Ⓐ Ⓑ Ⓒ Ⓓ Ⓔ	23	Ⓐ Ⓑ Ⓒ Ⓓ Ⓔ
4	Ⓐ Ⓑ Ⓒ Ⓓ Ⓔ	14	Ⓐ Ⓑ Ⓒ Ⓓ Ⓔ	24	Ⓐ Ⓑ Ⓒ Ⓓ Ⓔ
5	Ⓐ Ⓑ Ⓒ Ⓓ Ⓔ	15	Ⓐ Ⓑ Ⓒ Ⓓ Ⓔ	25	Ⓐ Ⓑ Ⓒ Ⓓ Ⓔ
6	Ⓐ Ⓑ Ⓒ Ⓓ Ⓔ	16	Ⓐ Ⓑ Ⓒ Ⓓ Ⓔ		
7	Ⓐ Ⓑ Ⓒ Ⓓ Ⓔ	17	Ⓐ Ⓑ Ⓒ Ⓓ Ⓔ		
8	Ⓐ Ⓑ Ⓒ Ⓓ Ⓔ	18	Ⓐ Ⓑ Ⓒ Ⓓ Ⓔ		
9	Ⓐ Ⓑ Ⓒ Ⓓ Ⓔ	19	Ⓐ Ⓑ Ⓒ Ⓓ Ⓔ		
10	Ⓐ Ⓑ Ⓒ Ⓓ Ⓔ	20	Ⓐ Ⓑ Ⓒ Ⓓ Ⓔ		

SSAT Middle Level Math

Practice Test 1

Section 1

25 questions

Total time for this test: 30 Minutes

You may NOT use a calculator on this part.

1. If 30 percent of a number is 60, then 20 percent of the same number is …
   (A) 12
   (B) 18
   (C) 25
   (D) 30
   (E) 40

2. Which of the following is NOT equal to 2×0.4?
   (A) 4×0.2
   (B) 1×0.8
   (C) $\frac{16}{8} \times \frac{4}{10}$
   (D) $\frac{5}{15} \times 3$
   (E) 0.8×1

3. Sara has M books. Mary has 6 more books than Sara. If Mary gives Sara 4 books, how many books will Mary have, in terms of M?
   (A) M
   (B) $M + 1$
   (C) $M + 2$
   (D) $M + 6$
   (E) $M - 6$

4. If $\frac{x}{2} = 30$, then $\frac{3x}{2} = ?$
   (A) 10
   (B) 20
   (C) 30
   (D) 45
   (E) 90

5. Which of the following is closest to $\frac{1}{6}$ of 40?
   (A) 0.3×6
   (B) 0.3×5
   (C) 0.2×30
   (D) 0.2×35
   (E) 0.2×39.5

6. What is the area of a square whose diagonal is 8?
   (A) 16
   (B) 32
   (C) 36
   (D) 64
   (E) 80

7. An angle is equal to one fifth of its supplement. What is the measure of that angle?
   (A) 20
   (B) 30
   (C) 45
   (D) 60
   (E) 150

8. A $44 shirt now selling for $28 is discounted by approximately what percent?
   (A) 20%
   (B) 36%
   (C) 40%
   (D) 60%
   (E) 80%

9. 6 liters of water are poured into an aquarium that's $25cm$ long, $5cm$ wide, and $60cm$ high. How many centimeters will the water level in the aquarium rise due to this added water?
   ($1\ liter\ of\ water = 1,000\ cm^3$)
   (A) 80
   (B) 48
   (C) 20
   (D) 10
   (E) 8

10. The perimeter of the trapezoid below is 64. What is its area?
    (A) $260\ cm^2$
    (B) $234\ cm^2$
    (C) $216\ cm^2$
    (D) $130\ cm^2$
    (E) $108cm^2$

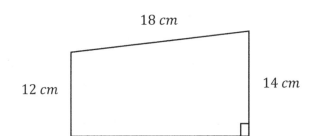

11. The score of Emma was half as that of Ava and the score of Mia was twice that of Ava. If the score of Mia was 40, what is the score of Emma?
    (A) 10
    (B) 18
    (C) 20
    (D) 30
    (E) 32

12. Two third of 9 is equal to $\frac{2}{5}$ of what number?

   (A) 60
   (B) 20
   (C) 15
   (D) 30
   (E) 36

13. If three times a number added to 5 equals to 32, what is the number?

   (A) 2
   (B) 4
   (C) 6
   (D) 9
   (E) 10

14. Solve for x: $4(x + 1) = 6(x - 4) + 20$

   (A) 12
   (B) 6.5
   (C) 4
   (D) 2
   (E) 1

15. Karen is 9 years older than her sister Michelle, and Michelle is 4 years younger than her brother David. If the sum of their ages is 82, how old is Michelle?

   (A) 14
   (B) 23
   (C) 22
   (D) 25
   (E) 30

16. Two-kilograms apple and two-kilograms orange cost $26.4. If one-kilogram apple costs $4.2 how much does one-kilogram orange cost?

   (A) $9
   (B) $6
   (C) $5.5
   (D) $5
   (E) $4.5

17. The average weight of 18 girls in a class is 50 kg and the average weight of 32 boys in the same class is 62 kg. What is the average weight of all the 50 students in that class?
   (A) 57.68
   (B) 61.68
   (C) 61.90
   (D) 62.20
   (E) 64.00

18. What is the value of x in this equation? $6(x + 4) = 78$
   (A) 4
   (B) 6
   (C) 9
   (D) 10
   (E) 12

19. When a number is subtracted from 32 and the difference is divided by that number, the result is 3. What is the value of the number?

   (A) 2
   (B) 4
   (C) 8
   (D) 12
   (E) 15

20. Which is the correct statement?
   (A) $\frac{3}{4} > 0.8$
   (B) $10\% = \frac{2}{5}$
   (C) $3 < \frac{5}{2}$
   (D) $\frac{5}{6} > 0.8$
   (E) $2.5\% = 0.25$

21. In a group of 5 books, the average number of pages is 24. Mary adds a book with 36 pages to the group. What is the new average number of pages per book?
   (A) 20
   (B) 22
   (C) 24
   (D) 26
   (E) 30

22. A football team won exactly 70% of the games it played during last session. Which of the following could be the total number of games the team played last season?
    (A) 49
    (B) 40
    (C) 32
    (D) 12
    (E) 9

23. If a gas tank can hold 35 gallons, how many gallons does it contain when it is $\frac{2}{5}$ full?
    (A) 50
    (B) 125
    (C) 62.5
    (D) 14
    (E) 8

24. What is the value of x in the following figure? (Figure is not drawn to scale)
    (A) 150
    (B) 145
    (C) 125
    (D) 105
    (E) 85

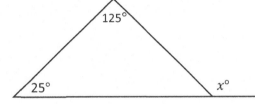

25. The capacity of a red box is 20% bigger than the capacity of a blue box. If 36 books can be put in the red box, how many books can be put in the blue box?

    (A) 15
    (B) 20
    (C) 24
    (D) 30
    (E) 32

IF YOU FINISH BEFORE TIME IS CALLED, YOU MAY CHECK YOUR WORK ON THIS SECTION ONLY. DO NOT TURN TO OTHER SECTION IN THE TEST. **STOP**

SSAT Middle Level Math

Practice Test 1

Section 2

25 questions

Total time for this test: 30 Minutes

You may NOT use a calculator on this part.

1. A taxi driver earns $8 per 1-hour work. If he works 10 hours a day and in 1 hour he uses 2-liters petrol with price $1 for 1-liter. How much money does he earn in one day?
   (A) $90
   (B) $88
   (C) $70
   (D) $60
   (E) $56

2. Which of the following is less than $\frac{1}{5}$?
   (A) $\frac{1}{4}$
   (B) 0.5
   (C) $\frac{1}{7}$
   (D) 0.28
   (E) 0.31

3. Amy and John work in a same company. Last month, both of them received a raise of 20 percent. If Amy earns $30.00 per hour now and John earns $28.80, Amy earned how much more per hour than John before their raises?
   (A) $8.25
   (B) $4.25
   (C) $3.00
   (D) $2.25
   (E) $1.00

4. Three people can paint 3 houses in 12 days. How many people are needed to paint 6 houses in 6 days?
   (A) 6
   (B) 8
   (C) 12
   (D) 16
   (E) 20

5. If $N \times (6 - 3) = 12$ then $N =$?
   (A) 4
   (B) 12
   (C) 13
   (D) 14
   (E) 18

6. The length of a rectangle is 3 times of its width. If the length is 24, what is the perimeter of the rectangle?
   (A) 24
   (B) 30
   (C) 36
   (D) 48
   (E) 64

7. In the figure below, what is the value of x? (Figure is not drawn to scale)
   (A) 43
   (B) 72
   (C) 77
   (D) 90
   (E) 98

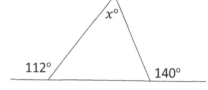

8. If $x \blacksquare y = 4x + y - 2$, what is the value of $4 \blacksquare 12$?
   (A) 4
   (B) 18
   (C) 26
   (D) 36
   (E) 48

9. The width of a rectangle is $4x$, the length is $6x$, and the perimeter of the rectangle is 90. What is the value of x?
   (A) 1
   (B) 2.2
   (C) 3
   (D) 4.5
   (E) 5.8

10. How many tiles of $8\ cm^2$ is needed to cover a floor of dimension $7\ cm$ by $24\ cm$?
    (A) 6
    (B) 12
    (C) 21
    (D) 24
    (E) 30

11. If 0.65 equals $65M$, what is the value of M?
    (A) 0.10
    (B) 0.01
    (C) 1.00
    (D) 11.01
    (E) 0.11

12. If $z = 3x + 5$, what does $2z + 3$ equal?
   (A) $6x + 6$
   (B) $6x + 12$
   (C) $6x - 12$
   (D) $6x - 6$
   (E) $6x + 13$

13. If 96 is the product of 4 and $8x$, then 96 is divisible by which of the following?
   (A) $x + 4$
   (B) $2x - 1$
   (C) $5x - 3$
   (D) $x \times 3$
   (E) $3x + 1$

$$0.0ABC \qquad\qquad 0.0D$$

14. The letters represent two decimals listed above. One of the decimals is equivalent to $\frac{1}{16}$ and the other is equivalent to $\frac{1}{25}$. What is the product of C and D?
   (A) 0
   (B) 5
   (C) 25
   (D) 20
   (E) 40

15. $\frac{x}{x-2} = \frac{4}{5}$, $x - 5 =$?
   (A) -13
   (B) -15
   (C) -17
   (D) 12
   (E) 15

16. A company pays its employer $7,000 plus 3% of all sales profit. If x is the number of all sales profit, which of the following represents the employer's revenue?

   (A) $0.03x$
   (B) $0.97x - 7,000$
   (C) $0.03x + 7,000$
   (D) $0.97x + 7,000$
   (E) $0.3x + 7,000$

17. In a certain bookshelf of a library, there are 35 biology books, 85 history books, and 90 language books. What is the ratio of the number of biology books to the total number of books in this bookshelf?

(A) $\frac{1}{4}$

(B) $\frac{1}{6}$

(C) $\frac{2}{7}$

(D) $\frac{3}{8}$

(E) $\frac{1}{4}$

18. If $5,000 + A - 200 = 7,400$, then $A = \cdots$
    (A) 200
    (B) 600
    (C) 1,600
    (D) 2,600
    (E) 3,000

19. The circle graph below shows all Mr. Green's expenses for last month. If he spent $770 on his car, how much did he spend for his rent?
    (A) $700
    (B) $740
    (C) $780
    (D) $810
    (E) $945

Mr. Green's monthly expenses

20. If $5 \times M + 3 = 5$, M equals to ….
    (A) 2
    (B) 4
    (C) $\frac{2}{5}$
    (D) 6
    (E) $\frac{1}{3}$

21. Which of the following is equal to $\frac{52.6}{100}$?
    (A) 52.6
    (B) 5.26
    (C) 526.0
    (D) 0.0526
    (E) 0.526

22. In the following figure, point Q lies on line A, what is the value of y if $x = 28$? (Figure is not drawn to scale)
(A) 32
(B) 37
(C) 42
(D) 45
(E) 56

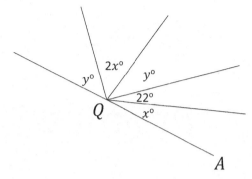

23. A container holds 2.5 gallons of water when it is $\frac{5}{24}$ full. How many gallons of water does the container hold when it's full?
(A) 8
(B) 12
(C) 16
(D) 20
(E) 30

24. At a Zoo, the ratio of lions to tigers is 3 to 1. Which of the following could NOT be the total number of lions and tigers in the zoo?
(A) 64
(B) 80
(C) 98
(D) 104
(E) 160

25. If x is greater than 18, then $\frac{1}{3}$ of x must be...
(A) Greater than 3
(B) Greater than 6
(C) Equal to 6
(D) Equal to 3
(E) Less than 3

IF YOU FINISH BEFORE TIME IS CALLED, YOU MAY CHECK YOUR WORK ON THIS SECTION ONLY. DO NOT TURN TO ANY OTHER SECTION IN THE TEST. **STOP**

SSAT Middle Level Math

Practice Test 2

2020 - 2021

Two Parts

Total number of questions: 50

Section 1: 25 questions

Section 2: 25 questions

Total time for two parts: 60 Minutes

SSAT Practice Test 2 Answer Sheet

Remove (or photocopy) this answer sheet and use it to complete the practice test.

SSAT Middle Level Mathematics Practice Test 2 Answer Sheet

SSAT Middle Level Practice Test 2 Section 1

1	Ⓐ Ⓑ Ⓒ Ⓓ Ⓔ	11 Ⓐ Ⓑ Ⓒ Ⓓ Ⓔ	21 Ⓐ Ⓑ Ⓒ Ⓓ Ⓔ
2	Ⓐ Ⓑ Ⓒ Ⓓ Ⓔ	12 Ⓐ Ⓑ Ⓒ Ⓓ Ⓔ	22 Ⓐ Ⓑ Ⓒ Ⓓ Ⓔ
3	Ⓐ Ⓑ Ⓒ Ⓓ Ⓔ	13 Ⓐ Ⓑ Ⓒ Ⓓ Ⓔ	23 Ⓐ Ⓑ Ⓒ Ⓓ Ⓔ
4	Ⓐ Ⓑ Ⓒ Ⓓ Ⓔ	14 Ⓐ Ⓑ Ⓒ Ⓓ Ⓔ	24 Ⓐ Ⓑ Ⓒ Ⓓ Ⓔ
5	Ⓐ Ⓑ Ⓒ Ⓓ Ⓔ	15 Ⓐ Ⓑ Ⓒ Ⓓ Ⓔ	25 Ⓐ Ⓑ Ⓒ Ⓓ Ⓔ
6	Ⓐ Ⓑ Ⓒ Ⓓ Ⓔ	16 Ⓐ Ⓑ Ⓒ Ⓓ Ⓔ	
7	Ⓐ Ⓑ Ⓒ Ⓓ Ⓔ	17 Ⓐ Ⓑ Ⓒ Ⓓ Ⓔ	
8	Ⓐ Ⓑ Ⓒ Ⓓ Ⓔ	18 Ⓐ Ⓑ Ⓒ Ⓓ Ⓔ	
9	Ⓐ Ⓑ Ⓒ Ⓓ Ⓔ	19 Ⓐ Ⓑ Ⓒ Ⓓ Ⓔ	
10	Ⓐ Ⓑ Ⓒ Ⓓ Ⓔ	20 Ⓐ Ⓑ Ⓒ Ⓓ Ⓔ	

SSAT Middle Level Practice Test 2 Section 2

1	Ⓐ Ⓑ Ⓒ Ⓓ Ⓔ	11 Ⓐ Ⓑ Ⓒ Ⓓ Ⓔ	21 Ⓐ Ⓑ Ⓒ Ⓓ Ⓔ
2	Ⓐ Ⓑ Ⓒ Ⓓ Ⓔ	12 Ⓐ Ⓑ Ⓒ Ⓓ Ⓔ	22 Ⓐ Ⓑ Ⓒ Ⓓ Ⓔ
3	Ⓐ Ⓑ Ⓒ Ⓓ Ⓔ	13 Ⓐ Ⓑ Ⓒ Ⓓ Ⓔ	23 Ⓐ Ⓑ Ⓒ Ⓓ Ⓔ
4	Ⓐ Ⓑ Ⓒ Ⓓ Ⓔ	14 Ⓐ Ⓑ Ⓒ Ⓓ Ⓔ	24 Ⓐ Ⓑ Ⓒ Ⓓ Ⓔ
5	Ⓐ Ⓑ Ⓒ Ⓓ Ⓔ	15 Ⓐ Ⓑ Ⓒ Ⓓ Ⓔ	25 Ⓐ Ⓑ Ⓒ Ⓓ Ⓔ
6	Ⓐ Ⓑ Ⓒ Ⓓ Ⓔ	16 Ⓐ Ⓑ Ⓒ Ⓓ Ⓔ	
7	Ⓐ Ⓑ Ⓒ Ⓓ Ⓔ	17 Ⓐ Ⓑ Ⓒ Ⓓ Ⓔ	
8	Ⓐ Ⓑ Ⓒ Ⓓ Ⓔ	18 Ⓐ Ⓑ Ⓒ Ⓓ Ⓔ	
9	Ⓐ Ⓑ Ⓒ Ⓓ Ⓔ	19 Ⓐ Ⓑ Ⓒ Ⓓ Ⓔ	
10	Ⓐ Ⓑ Ⓒ Ⓓ Ⓔ	20 Ⓐ Ⓑ Ⓒ Ⓓ Ⓔ	

SSAT Middle Level Math

Practice Test 2

Section 1

25 questions

Total time for this test: 30 Minutes

You may NOT use a calculator on this part.

1. How long does a 420–miles trip take moving at 65 miles per hour (mph)?
   (A) 4 *hours*
   (B) 6 *hours and* 24 *minutes*
   (C) 8 *hours and* 24 *minutes*
   (D) 8 *hours and* 30 *minutes*
   (E) 10 *hours and* 30 *minutes*

2. The marked price of a computer is D dollar. Its price decreased by 15% in January and later increased by 10% in February. What is the final price of the computer in D dollar?
   (A) 0.80 D
   (B) 0.88 D
   (C) 0.93 D
   (D) 1.20 D
   (E) 1.40 D

3. If 0.35 equals 350M, what is the value of M?
   (A) 0.001
   (B) 0.01
   (C) 1.0
   (D) 1.01
   (E) 1.001

4. Jason borrowed $5,800 for three months at an annual rate of 5%. How much interest did Jason owe?
   (A) $45
   (B) $72.50
   (C) $120
   (D) $240
   (E) $480

5. If three times a certain number, increased by 10, is equal to 40, what is the number?
   (A) 10
   (B) 12
   (C) 18
   (D) 27
   (E) 54

6. If 30 percent of a number is 150, then 15 percent of the same number is ?
   (A) 75
   (B) 79
   (C) 80
   (D) 90
   (E) 120

7. The average of $13, 15, 20$ and x is 20. What is the value of x?
   (A) 9
   (B) 15
   (C) 18
   (D) 20
   (E) 32

8. In five successive hours, a car traveled $40\ km, 45\ km, 50\ km, 35\ km$ and $55\ km$. In the next five hours, it traveled with an average speed of $55\ km\ per\ hour$. Find the total distance the car traveled in 10 hours.
   (A) $425\ km$
   (B) $450\ km$
   (C) $475\ km$
   (D) $500\ km$
   (E) $1,000\ km$

9. John has N toy cars. Jack has 6 more cars than John. If Jack gives John 3 cars, how many cars will Jack have, in terms of N?
   (A) N
   (B) $N - 1$
   (C) $N + 1$
   (D) $N + 2$
   (E) $N + 3$

10. What is the value of x in the following equation?
$$\frac{x + 4}{5} = 3$$
   (A) 2
   (B) 4
   (C) 6
   (D) 8
   (E) 11

11. The ratio of boys to girls in a school is $2 : 3$. If there are 500 students in a school, how many boys are in the school.
   (A) 540
   (B) 360
   (C) 300
   (D) 280
   (E) 200

12. Two third of 24 is equal to $\frac{2}{5}$ of what number?

    (A) 12

    (B) 20

    (C) 40

    (D) 60

    (E) 90

13. What is the cost of seven ounces of cheese at $0.96 *per pound*?

    (A) $0.42

    (B) $0.45

    (C) $0.48

    (D) $0.52

    (E) $0.64

14. If 60% of A is 30% of B, then B is what percent of A?

    (A) 3%

    (B) 30%

    (C) 200%

    (D) 300%

    (E) 900%

15. Sophia purchased a sofa for $504. The sofa is regularly priced at $600. What was the percent discount Sophia received on the sofa?

    (A) 12%

    (B) 16%

    (C) 20%

    (D) 25%

    (E) 40%

16. A bag contains 18 balls: two green, five black, eight blue, a brown, a red and one white. If 17 balls are removed from the bag at random, what is the probability that a brown ball has been removed?

    (A) $\frac{1}{9}$

    (B) $\frac{1}{18}$

    (C) $\frac{16}{17}$

    (D) $\frac{17}{18}$

    (E) $\frac{1}{2}$

17. When a number is subtracted from 28 and the difference is divided by that number, the result is 3. What is the value of the number?
   (A) 2
   (B) 4
   (C) 7
   (D) 12
   (E) 24

18. If 45% of a class are girls, and 25% of girls play tennis, approximately what percent of the class play tennis?
   (A) 11%
   (B) 15%
   (C) 20%
   (D) 40%
   (E) 80%

19. 44 students took an exam and 11 of them failed. What percent of the students passed the exam?
   (A) 20%
   (B) 40%
   (C) 60%
   (D) 75%
   (E) 90%

20. What is the value of x in the following equation?
$$3x + 10 = 67$$
   (A) 5
   (B) 7
   (C) 9
   (D) 11
   (E) 19

21. If $N \times \frac{4}{3} \times 7 = 0$, then $N = ...$
   (A) 0
   (B) 1
   (C) 2
   (D) 3
   (E) 4

22. Jason left a $12.00 tip on a lunch that cost $60.00, approximately what percentage was the tip?

(A) 2.5%
(B) 10%
(C) 15%
(D) 20%
(E) 25%

23. If 60% of a number is 6, what is the number?

(A) 4
(B) 8
(C) 10
(D) 12
(E) 20

24. If $\frac{z}{5} = 4$, then $z + 3 =$?

(A) 4
(B) 5
(C) 15
(D) 20
(E) 23

25. In 1999, the average worker's income increased $3,000 per year starting from $24,000 annual salary. Which equation represents income greater than average? (I = income, x = number of years after 1999)

(A) $I > 3,000x + 24,000$
(B) $I > -3,000x + 24,000$
(C) $I < -3,000x + 24,000$
(D) $I < 3,000x - 24,000$
(E) $I < 24,000x + 24,000$

IF YOU FINISH BEFORE TIME IS CALLED, YOU MAY CHECK YOUR WORK ON THIS SECTION ONLY. DO NOT TURN TO ANY OTHER SECTION IN THE TEST. **STOP**

SSAT Middle Level Math

Practice Test 2

Section 2

25 questions

Total time for this test: 30 Minutes

You may NOT use a calculator on this part.

1. John has x dollars and he receives $150. He then buys a bicycle that costs $110. How much money does John have now?
   (A) $x + 150$
   (B) $x + 110$
   (C) $x + 40$
   (D) $x - 120$
   (E) $x - 40$

2. What is the value of x in this equation?
$$\frac{x - 3}{8} + 5 = 20$$
   (A) 131
   (B) 128
   (C) 123
   (D) 120
   (E) 115

3. Bob needs an 78% average in his writing class to pass. On his first 4 exams, he earned scores of 68%, 72%, 85%, and 90%. What is the minimum score Bob can earn on his fifth and final test to pass?
   (A) 80%,
   (B) 75%
   (C) 68%
   (D) 64%
   (E) 60%

4. The width of a rectangle is $6x$, the length is $8x$, and the perimeter is 84. What is the value of x?
   (A) 1
   (B) 2
   (C) 3
   (D) 4
   (E) 5

5. A bank is offering 3.5% simple interest on a savings account. If you deposit $8,000, how much interest will you earn in five years?
   (A) $360
   (B) $720
   (C) $1,400
   (D) $3,600
   (E) $4,800

6. If $(8 - 4) \times 4 = 8 + \square$, then $\square = ?$
   (A) 5
   (B) 6
   (C) 7
   (D) 8
   (E) 9

7. Jason is 9 miles ahead of Joe running at 6.5 miles per hour and Joe is running at the speed of 8 miles per hour. How long does it take Joe to catch Jason?
   (A) 3 *hours*
   (B) 4 *hours*
   (C) 6 *hours*
   (D) 8 *hours*
   (E) 10 *hours*

8. In a classroom, there are y tables that can each seat 4 people and there are x tables that can each seat 8 people. What is the number of people that can be seated in the classroom?
   (A) $4y$
   (B) $8x$
   (C) $8x - 4y$
   (D) 13
   (E) $8x + 4y$

9. The area of a circle is 81π. What is the diameter of the circle?
   (A) 4
   (B) 8
   (C) 12
   (D) 14
   (E) 18

10. A shirt costing $300 is discounted 15%. After a month, the shirt is discounted another 15%. Which of the following expressions can be used to find the selling price of the shirt?
    (A) $(300)\,(0.70)$
    (B) $(300) - 300\,(0.30)$
    (C) $(300)(0.15) - (300)\,(0.15)$
    (D) $(300)\,(0.85)\,(0.85)$
    (E) $(300)(0.85)(0.85) - (300)\,(0.15)$

11. Four one – foot rulers can be split among how many users to leave each with $\frac{1}{3}$ of a ruler?
    (A) 4
    (B) 6
    (C) 12
    (D) 24
    (E) 48

124

12. The perimeter of a rectangular yard is 72 meters. What is its length if its width is twice its length?

    (A) 12 $meters$

    (B) 18 $meters$

    (C) 20 $meters$

    (D) 24 $meters$

    (E) 36 $meters$

13. What is the value of x in this equation? $2x + 10 = 48$

    (A) 19

    (B) 14

    (C) 12

    (D) 10

    (E) 6

14. The mean of 50 test scores was calculated as 86. But, it turned out that one of the scores was misread as 94 but it was 69. What is the mean?

    (A) 85.5

    (B) 85

    (C) 84.5

    (D) 83.5

    (E) 80.5

15. The average of 6 numbers is 15. The average of 4 of those numbers is 10. What is the average of the other two numbers?

    (A) 10

    (B) 12

    (C) 14

    (D) 15

    (E) 25

16. If $x + 5 = 8$, $2y - 1 = 5$ then $xy + 15 =$

    (A) 10

    (B) 19

    (C) 24

    (D) 27

    (E) 32

17. A card is drawn at random from a standard 52–card deck, what is the probability that the card is of Hearts? (The deck includes 13 of each suit clubs, diamonds, hearts, and spades)

(A) $\frac{1}{3}$

(B) $\frac{1}{4}$

(C) $\frac{1}{6}$

(D) $\frac{1}{52}$

(E) $\frac{1}{104}$

18. Which of the following is NOT less than $\frac{1}{5}$?

(A) $\frac{1}{8}$

(B) $\frac{1}{3}$

(C) $\frac{1}{9}$

(D) 0.14

(E) 17%

19. Mr. Jones saves $2,500 out of his monthly family income of $65,000. What fractional part of his income does he save?

(A) $\frac{1}{26}$

(B) $\frac{1}{11}$

(C) $\frac{3}{25}$

(D) $\frac{2}{15}$

(E) $\frac{1}{15}$

20. If $5x - 6 = 39$, then $3x + 6 =$?

(A) 18

(B) 20

(C) 22

(D) 33

(E) 36

21. In two successive years, the population of a town is increased by 10% and 20%. What percent of the population is increased after two years?

(A) 32%

(B) 31%

(C) 30%

(D) 28%

(E) 22%

22. If 150% of a number is 75, then what is the 80% of that number?
   (A) 40
   (B) 50
   (C) 70
   (D) 85
   (E) 90

23. What is the equivalent temperature of $140°F$ in Celsius? ($C = Celsius$)
$$C = \frac{5}{9} (F - 32)$$

   (A) 32
   (B) 40
   (C) 48
   (D) 52
   (E) 60

24. The perimeter of the trapezoid below is $50 \ cm$. What is its area?

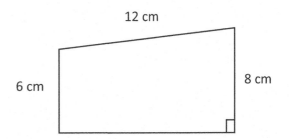

   (A) $48 \ cm^2$
   (B) $70 \ cm^2$
   (C) $168 \ cm^2$
   (D) $576 \ cm^2$
   (E) $986 \ cm^2$

25. The width of a box is one third of its length. The height of the box is half of its width. If the length of the box is $24 \ cm$, what is the volume of the box?
   (A) $81 \ cm^3$
   (B) $162 \ cm^3$
   (C) $243 \ cm^3$
   (D) $768 \ cm^3$
   (E) $1880 \ cm^3$

IF YOU FINISH BEFORE TIME IS CALLED, YOU MAY CHECK YOUR WORK ON THIS SECTION ONLY. DO NOT TURN TO OTHER SECTION IN THE TEST. | STOP

SSAT Middle Level Math Practice Test Answers and Explanations

Now, it's time to review your results to see where you went wrong and what areas you need to improve

SSAT Middle Level Math Practice Test 1								SSAT Middle Level Math Practice Test 2							
Section 1				**Section 2**				**Section 1**				**Section 2**			
1	E	16	A	1	D	16	C	1	B	16	D	1	C	16	C
2	D	17	A	2	C	17	B	2	C	17	C	2	C	17	B
3	C	18	C	3	E	18	D	3	A	18	A	3	B	18	B
4	E	19	C	4	C	19	E	4	B	19	D	4	C	19	A
5	D	20	D	5	A	20	C	5	A	20	E	5	C	20	D
6	B	21	D	6	E	21	E	6	A	21	A	6	D	21	A
7	B	22	B	7	B	22	B	7	E	22	D	7	C	22	A
8	B	23	D	8	C	23	B	8	D	23	C	8	E	23	E
9	B	24	A	9	D	24	C	9	E	24	E	9	E	24	C
10	A	25	D	10	C	25	B	10	E	25	A	10	D	25	D
11	A			11	B			11	E			11	C		
12	C			12	E			12	C			12	A		
13	D			13	C			13	A			13	A		
14	C			14	D			14	C			14	A		
15	B			15	A			15	B			15	E		

Score Your Test

SSAT scores are broken down by its three sections: Verbal, Mathematics, and Reading. A sum of the three sections is also reported.

For the Middle Level SSAT, the score range is 500-800, the lowest possible score a student can earn is 500 and the highest score is 800 for each section. A student receives 1 point for every correct answer and loses $\frac{1}{4}$ point for each incorrect answer. No points are lost by skipping a question.

The total scaled score for a Middle Level SSAT test is the sum of the scores for the Mathematics, verbal, and reading sections. A student will also receive a percentile score of between 1-99% that compares that student's test scores with those of other test takers of same grade and gender from the past 3 years.

Use the following table to convert SSAT Middle level raw score to scaled score.

SSAT Middle Level Math Scaled Scores	
Raw Scores	Mathematics
50	710
45	680
40	660
35	635
30	615
25	590
20	570
15	540
10	525
5	500
0	480
-5	460
- 10 and lower	440

SSAT Middle Level Mathematics Practice Test 1 Section 1

1) Choice E is correct

If 30 percent of a number is 60, then the number is: $30\% \ of \ x = 60 \rightarrow 0.3x = 60 \rightarrow x = \frac{60}{0.3} = \frac{600}{3} = 200$, 20 percent of 200 is: $20\% \ of \ 200 = \frac{20}{100} \times 200 = 40$

2) Choice D is correct

$2 \times 0.4 = 0.8$, all **choices** provided are equal to 0.8 except option D. $\frac{5}{15} \times 3 = 1$

3) Choice C is correct

Sara has M books. Mary has 6 more books than Sara. Then, Mary has $M + 6$ books. If Mary gives Sara 4 books, Mary will have: $M + 6 - 4 = M + 2$

4) Choice E is correct

If $\frac{x}{2} = 30$, then $\frac{3x}{2}$ is 3 times $\frac{x}{2}$. The answer is 90.

5) Choice D is correct

$\frac{1}{6}$ of 40 is 6.66. Let's review the **choices** provided:

(A) $0.3 \times 6 = 1.8$
(B) $0.3 \times 5 = 1.5$
(C) $0.2 \times 30 = 6$
(D) $0.2 \times 35 = 7$
(E) $0.2 \times 39.5 = 7.9$

Option D is the closest to 6.66

6) Choice B is correct

The diagonal of the square is 8. Let x be the side.

Use Pythagorean Theorem: $a^2 + b^2 = c^2$

$x^2 + x^2 = 8^2 \Rightarrow 2x^2 = 8^2 \Rightarrow 2x^2 = 64 \Rightarrow x^2 = 32 \Rightarrow x = \sqrt{32}$

The area of the square is: $\sqrt{32} \times \sqrt{32} = 32$

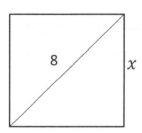

7) Choice B is correct

The sum of supplement angles is 180. Let x be that angle. Therefore, $x + 5x = 180$

$6x = 180$, divide both sides by 6: $x = 30$

8) Choice B is correct

Use the formula for Percent of Change: $\dfrac{\text{New Value} - \text{Ol} \quad \text{Value}}{\text{Old Value}} \times 100\%$

$\dfrac{28-}{44} \times 100\% \approx -36\%$ (negative sign here means that the new price is less than old price)

9) Choice B is correct

$One\ liter = 1{,}000\ cm^3 \rightarrow 6\ liters = 6{,}000 cm^3\ ,\ 6{,}000 = 25 \times 5 \times h \rightarrow h = \dfrac{6{,}000}{125} = 48\ cm$

10) Choice A is correct

The perimeter of the trapezoid is 64.

Therefore, the missing side (height) is $= 64 - 18 - 12 - 14 = 20$

Area of the trapezoid: $A = \frac{1}{2}\,h\,(b_1 + b_2) = \frac{1}{2}\,(10)\,(12 + 14) = 260$

11) Choice A is correct

If the score of Mia was 40, therefore the score of Ava is 20. Since, the score of Emma was half as that of Ava, therefore, the score of Emma is 10.

12) Choice C is correct

Let x be the number. Write the equation and solve for x. $\frac{2}{3} \times 9 = \frac{2}{5} \cdot x \Rightarrow \frac{2 \times 9}{3} = \frac{2x}{5}$, use cross multiplication to solve for x. $5 \times 18 = 2x \times 3 \Rightarrow 90 = 6x \Rightarrow x = 15$

13) Choice D is correct

Let x be the number. Then: $3x + 5 = 32$ Solve for x: $3x + 5 = 32 \rightarrow 3x = 32 - 5 = 27 \rightarrow$

$$x = 27 \div 3 = 9$$

14) Choice C is correct

Simplify and solve for x in the equation. $4(x + 1) = 6(x - 4) + 20$, $4x + 4 = 6x - 24 + 20$, $4x + 4 = 6x - 4$. Subtract $4x$ from both sides: $4 = 2x - 4$, Add 4 to both sides: $8 = 2x$, $4 = x$

15) Choice B is correct

Let's write equations based on the information provided:

$Michelle = Karen - 9, Michelle = David - 4,\ Karen + Michelle + David = 82$

$Karen - 9 = Michelle \Rightarrow Karen = Michelle + 9$

$Karen + Michelle + David = 82$

Now, replace the ages of Karen and David by Michelle. Then:

$Michelle + 9 + Michelle + Michelle + 4 = 82$

$3 \times Michelle + 13 = 82 \Rightarrow 3 \times Michelle = 82 - 13$

$3 \times Michelle = 69 , Michelle = 23$

16) Choice A is correct

Let x be one-kilogram orange cost, then: $2x + (2 \times 4.2) = 26.4 \rightarrow 2x + 8.4 = 26.4 \rightarrow$

$$2x = 26.4 - 8.4 \rightarrow 2x = 18 \rightarrow x = \frac{18}{2} = \$9$$

17) Choice A is correct

$average = \frac{sum\ of\ terms}{number\ of\ terms}$, The sum of the weight of all girls is: $18 \times 50 = 900kg$, The sum of the weight of all boys is: $32 \times 62 = 1,984\ kg$, The sum of the weight of all students is:

$900 + 1,984 = 2,884\ kg, Average = \frac{2,884}{50} = 57.68$

18) Choice C is correct

Solve for x in the equation. $6(x + 4) = 78 \rightarrow 6x + 24 = 78 \rightarrow 6x = 78 - 24 = 54 \rightarrow$

$$x = 54 \div 6 = 9$$

19) Choice C is correct

Let x be the number. Write the equation and solve for x. $(32 - x) \div x = 3$
Multiply both sides by x. $(32 - x) = 3x$, then add x both sides. $32 = 4x$, now divide both sides by 4. $x = 8$

20) Choice D is correct

Only option D is correct. $\frac{5}{6} = 0.83 \rightarrow 0.8 < \frac{5}{6}$

21) Choice D is correct

In a group of 5 books, the average number of pages is 24. Therefore, the sum of pages in all 5 books is $(5 \times 24 = 120)$. Mary adds a book with 36 pages to the group. Then, the sum of pages in all 6 books is $(5 \times 24 + 36 = 156)$. The new average number of pages per book is: $\frac{156}{6} = 26$

22) Choice B is correct

Choices A, C, D, and E are incorrect because 70% of each of the numbers is a non-whole number.

A. 49, $70\%\ of\ 49 = 0.70 \times 49 = 34.3$
B. 40, $70\%\ of\ 40 = 0.70 \times 40 = 28$
C. 32, $70\%\ of\ 32 = 0.80 \times 32 = 22.4$
D. 12, $70\%\ of\ 12 = 0.70 \times 12 = 8.4$
E. 9, $70\%\ of\ 9 = 0.80 \times 9 = 6.3$

23) Choice D is correct

$$\frac{2}{5} \times 35 = \frac{70}{5} = 14$$

24) Choice A is correct

$$x = 25 + 125 = 150$$

25) Choice D is correct

The red box is 20% bigger than the blue box. Let x be the capacity of the blue box. Then:

$$x + 20\% \ of \ x = 36 \rightarrow 1.2x = 36 \rightarrow x = \frac{36}{1.2} = 30$$

SSAT Middle Level Mathematics Practice Test 1 Section 2

1) Choice D is correct

$\$8 \times 10 = \$80$, Petrol use: $10 \times 2 = 20$ liters, Petrol cost: $20 \times \$1 = \$20$

Money earned: $\$80 - \$20 = \$60$

2) Choice C is correct

From the **choices** provided, only C $(\frac{1}{7})$ is less than $\frac{1}{5}$.

3) Choice E is correct

Amy earns $\$30.00 \ per \ hour$ now. $\$30.00 \ per \ hour$ is 20 percent more than her previous rate. Let x be her rate before her raise. Then: $x + 0.20x = 30 \rightarrow 1.2x = 30 \rightarrow x = \frac{30}{1.2} = 25$

John earns $\$28.80 \ per \ hour$ now. $\$28.80 \ per \ hour$ is 20 percent more than his previous rate. Let x be John's rate before his raise. Then: $x + 0.20x = 28.80 \rightarrow 1.2x = 28.80 \rightarrow x = \frac{28.80}{1.2} = 24$, Amy earned $\$1.00$ more per hour than John before their raises.

4) Choice C is correct.

Three people can paint 3 houses in 12 days. It means that for painting 6 houses in 12 days we need 6 people. To paint 6 houses in 6 days, 12 people are needed.

5) Choice A is correct.

$N \times (6 - 3) = 12 \rightarrow N \times 3 = 12 \rightarrow N = 4$

6) Choice E is correct.

The length of the rectangle is 24. Then, its width is 8. $24 \div 3 = 8$

$Perimeter \ of \ a \ rectangle = 2 \times width + 2 \times length = 2 \times 8 + 2 \times 24 = 16 + 48 = 64$

7) Choice B is correct

Let write angles A and B in the figure. $A = 180° - 112° = 68°$, $B = 180° - 145° = 40°$

The sum of all angles in a triangle is 180 degrees. Then: $x + A + B = 180° \rightarrow$

$$x = 180° - 68° - 40° = 72°$$

8) Choice C is correct.

If $x \blacksquare y = 4x + y - 2$, Then: $4 \blacksquare 12 = 4(4) + 12 - 2 = 16 + 12 - 2 = 26$

9) Choice D is correct

The width of a rectangle is $4x$ and its length is $6x$. Therefore, the perimeter of the rectangle is $20x$. $Perimeter\ of\ a\ rectangle = 2(width + length) = 2(4x + 6x) = 2(10x) = 20x$

The perimeter of the rectangle is 90. Then: $20x = 90 \rightarrow x = 4.5$

10) Choice C is correct

The area of the floor is: $7\ cm \times 24\ cm = 168\ cm^2$, The number is tiles needed $= 168 \div 8 = 21$

11) Choice B is correct

0.65 equals $65M$. Then: $65M = 0.65 \rightarrow M = \frac{0.65}{65} = 0.01$

12) Choice E is correct

$z = 3x + 5$, then, $2z = 2(3x + 5) = 6x + 10$, $2z + 3 = 6x + 10 + 3 = 6x + 13$

13) Choice C is correct.

$96 = 8x \times 4 \rightarrow x = 96 \div 4 = 24 \rightarrow x = 3$

x equals to 3. Let's review the choices provided:
A) $x + 4 \rightarrow 3 + 4 = 7$ 96 is not divisible by 9.
B) $2x - 4 \rightarrow 2 \times 3 - 1 = 5$ 96 is not divisible by 5.
C) $5x - 3 \rightarrow 5 \times 3 - 3 = 12$ 96 is divisible by 12.
D) $x \times 3 \rightarrow 3 \times 3 = 9$ 96 is not divisible by 9.
E) $3x + 1 \rightarrow 3 \times 3 + 1 = 10$ 96 is not divisible by 10.

The answer is C.

14) Choice D is correct

$\frac{1}{16} = 0.0625 \rightarrow C = 5$, $\frac{1}{25} = 0.04 \rightarrow D = 4 \rightarrow C \times D = 5 \times 4 = 20$

15) Choice A is correct

Use cross product to solve for x.

$\frac{x}{x-2} = \frac{4}{5} \rightarrow 5 \times x = 4 \times (x - 2) \rightarrow 5x = 4x - 8 \rightarrow x = -8, x - 5 = -8 - 5 = -13$

16) Choice C is correct

x is the number of all sales profit and 3% of it is: $3\% \times x = 0.03x$, Employer's revenue:

$$0.03x + 7,000$$

17) Choice B is correct

Number of biology book: 35, Total number of books; $35 + 85 + 90 = 210$

The ratio of the number of biology books to the total number of books is: $\dfrac{35}{210} = \dfrac{1}{6}$

18) Choice D is correct.

$5,000 + A - 200 = 7,400 \rightarrow 5,000 + A = 7,400 + 200 = 7,600 \rightarrow A = 7,600 - 5,000 = 2,600$

19) Choice E is correct

Let x be all expenses, then $\dfrac{22}{100}x = \$770 \rightarrow x = \dfrac{100 \times \$770}{22} = \$3,500$,

He spent for his rent: $\dfrac{27}{100} \times \$3,500 = \$945$

20) Choice C is correct

$5 \times M + 3 = 5 \rightarrow 5 \times M = 5 - 3 = 2 \rightarrow M = \dfrac{2}{5}$

21) Choice E is correct

$$\dfrac{52.6}{100} = 0.526$$

22) Choice B is correct

The angles on a straight line add up to 180 degrees. Then: $x + 22 + y + 2x + y = 180$, Then, $3x + 2y = 180 - 22 \rightarrow 3(28) + 2y = 158 \rightarrow 2y = 158 - 84 = 74 \rightarrow y = 37$

23) Choice B is correct

let x be the number of gallons of water the container holds when it is full.

Then; $\dfrac{5}{24}x = 2.5 \rightarrow x = \dfrac{24 \times 2.5}{5} = 12$

24) Choice C is correct.

The ratio of lions to tigers is 3 to 1 at the zoo. Therefore, total number of lions and tigers must be divisible by 4. From the choices provided, only 98 is not divisible by 4.

25) Choice B is correct

If x is greater than 18, then $\dfrac{1}{3}$ of x must be greater than: $\dfrac{1}{3} \times 18 = 6$.

SSAT Middle Level Mathematics Practice Test 2 Section 1

1) Choice B is correct

Use distance formula: $Distance = Rate \times time \Rightarrow 420 = 65 \times T$, divide both sides by 65. $420 \div 65 = T \Rightarrow T = 6.4 \ hours$. Change hours to minutes for the decimal part.

$$0.4 \ hours \ = \ 0.4 \times 60 = 24 \ minutes.$$

2) Choice C is correct

To find the discount, multiply the number by $(100\% - rate \ of \ discount)$. Therefore, for the first discount we get: $(D) \ (100\% - 15\%) = (D) \ (0.85) = 0.85 \ D$

For increase of 10%: $(0.85 \ D) \ (100\% + 10\%) = (0.85 \ D) \ (1.10) = 0.93 \ D = 93\% \ of \ D \ or \ 0.93D$

3) Choice A is correct

0.35 equals $350M$. Then: $0.35 = 350M \rightarrow M = \frac{0.35}{350} = 0.001$

4) Choice B is correct

Use simple interest formula: $I = prt$, (I = interest, p = principal, r = rate, t = time)

t is for one year. For 3 months, t is $\frac{1}{4}$ or 0.25. $I = (5,800)(0.05)(0.25) = 72.50$

5) Choice A is correct

Three times a certain number, increased by 10, is equal to 40. Write an equation and solve.

$$3x + 10 = 40 \rightarrow 3x = 40 - 10 = 30 \rightarrow x = \frac{30}{3} = 10$$

6) Choice A is correct

30 percent of a number is 150. Therefore, the number is 500. $0.30x = 150 \rightarrow x = \frac{150}{0.30} = 500$

15 percent of 500 is 75. $0.15 \times 500 = 75$

7) Choice E is correct

$$average = \frac{sum \ of \ terms}{number \ of \ terms} \Rightarrow 20 = \frac{13 + 15 + 20 + x}{4} \Rightarrow 80 = 48 + x \Rightarrow x = 32$$

8) Choice D is correct

Add the first 5 numbers. $40 + 45 + 50 + 35 + 55 = 225$

To find the distance traveled in the next 5 hours, multiply the average by number of hours.

$Distance = Average \times Rate = 55 \times 5 = 275$, Add both numbers. $275 + 225 = 500$

9) Choice E is correct

John has N toy cars. Jack has 6 more cars than John. Therefore, Jack has $N + 6$ toy cars. Jack gives John 3 cars. Now, Jack has $(N + 6 - 3) \ N + 3$ toy cars.

10) Choice E is correct

$\frac{x+4}{5} = 3 \rightarrow x + 4 = 3 \times 5 = 15 \rightarrow x = 15 - 4 = 11$

11) Choice E is correct

Th ratio of boy to girls is $2:3$. Therefore, there are 2 boys out of 5 students. To find the answer, first divide the total number of students by 5, then multiply the result by 2.

$500 \div 5 = 100 \Rightarrow 100 \times 2 = 200$

12) Choice C is correct

Let x be the number. Write the equation and solve for x. $\frac{2}{3} \times 24 = \frac{2}{5} . x \Rightarrow \frac{2 \times 24}{3} = \frac{2x}{5}$, use cross multiplication to solve for x. $5 \times 48 = 2x \times 3 \Rightarrow 240 = 6x \Rightarrow x = 40$

13) Choice A is correct

One pound of cheese costs \$0.96. *One pound* $= 16$ *ounces*, 16 ounces of cheese costs \$0.96. Then, 1 ounce of chees costs $(0.96 \div 16)$ \$0.06. 7 ounces of cheese costs $(7 \times \$0.06)$ \$0.42.

14) Choice C is correct

Write the equation and solve for B: $0.60A = 0.30B$, divide both sides by 0.30, then you will have $\frac{0.60}{0.30}A = B$, therefore: $B = 2A$, and B is 2 times of A or it's 200% of A.

15) Choice B is correct

$\frac{504}{600} = 0.84$. 504 is 84 percent of 600. So, the discount is 16%. $100\% - 16\% = 84\%$

16) Choice D is correct

If 17 balls are removed from the bag at random, there will be one ball in the bag. The probability of choosing a brown ball is 1 out of 18. Therefore, the probability of not choosing a brown ball is 17 out of 18 and the probability of having not a brown ball after removing 17 balls is the same.

17) Choice C is correct

Let x be the number. Write the equation and solve for x. $(28 - x) \div x = 3$. Multiply both sides by x. $(28 - x) = 3x$, then add x both sides. $28 = 4x$, now divide both sides by 4. $x = 7$

18) Choice A is correct

The percent of girls playing tennis is: $45\% \times 25\% = 0.45 \times 0.25 \approx 0.11 = 11\%$

19) Choice D is correct

The failing rate is 11 out of $44 = \frac{11}{55}$. Change the fraction to percent: $\frac{11}{44} \times 100\% = 25\%$

25 percent of students failed. Therefore, 75 percent of students passed the exam.

20) Choice E is correct

$$3x + 10 = 67 \rightarrow 3x = 67 - 10 = 57 \rightarrow x = \frac{57}{3} = 19$$

21) Choice A is correct

$N \times \frac{4}{3} \times 7 = 0$, then N must be 0.

22) Choice D is correct

$12 **is what percent of** $60? $12 \div 60 = 0.20 = 20\%$

23) Choice C is correct

Let x be the number. Write the equation and solve for x.

$60\% \; of \; x = 6 \Rightarrow 0.60 \; x = 6 \Rightarrow x = 6 \div 0.60 = 10$

24) Choice E is correct

$\frac{z}{5} = 4 \rightarrow z = 4 \times 5 = 20, z + 3 = 20 + 3 = 23$

25) Choice A is correct

Let x be the number of years. Therefore, \$3,000 per year equals $3000x$. starting from \$24,000 annual salary means you should add that amount to $2000x$. Income more than that is:

$I > 3000x + 24000$

SSAT Middle Level Mathematics Practice Test 2 Section 2

1) Choice C is correct

John has x dollars and he receives \$150. Therefore, he has $x + 150$.

He then buys a bicycle that costs \$110. Now, he has: $x + 150 - 110 = x + 40$

2) Choice C is correct

$$\frac{x-3}{8} + 5 = 20 \rightarrow \frac{x-3}{8} = 20 - 5 = 15 \rightarrow x - 3 = 15 \times 8 = 120 \rightarrow$$
$$x = 120 + 3 = 123$$

3) Choice B is correct

Bob needs an 78% average to pass for five exams. Therefore, the sum of 5 exams must be at lease $5 \times 78 = 390$, The sum of 4 exams is: $68 + 72 + 85 + 90 = 315$.

The minimum score Bob can earn on his fifth and final test to pass is: $390 - 315 = 75$

4) Choice C is correct

The width of a rectangle is $6x$ and its length is $8x$. Then, the perimeter of the rectangle is $28x$.

Perimeter of a rectangle $= 2(width + length) = 2(6x + 8x) = 28x$

The perimeter of the rectangle is 84. Then: $28x = 84 \rightarrow x = 3$

5) Choice C is correct

Use simple interest formula: $I = prt$, (I = interest, p = principal, r = rate, t = time)

$I = (8,000)(0.035)(5) = 1,400$

6) Choice D is correct

$(8 - 4) \times 4 = 8 + \square$

Then: $4 \times 4 = 8 + \square$, $16 = 8 + \square$, then $\square = 8$

7) Choice C is correct

The distance between Jason and Joe is 9 miles. Jason running at 6.5 miles per hour and Joe is running at the speed of 8 miles per hour. Therefore, every hour the distance is 1.5 miles less.

$9 \div 1.5 = 6$

8) Choice E is correct

There are y tables that can each seat 4 people and there are x tables that can each seat 8 people. Therefore, $4y + 8x$ people can be seated in the classroom

9) Choice E is correct

The formula for the area of the circle is: $A = \pi r^2$

The area of the circle is 81π. **Therefore:** $A = \pi r^2 \Rightarrow 81\pi = \pi r^2$, **Divide both sides by** π: $81 = r^2 \Rightarrow r = 9$, Diameter of a circle is $2 \times$ radius. Then: Diameter $= 2 \times 9 = 18$

10) Choice D is correct

To find the discount, multiply the number by $(100\% - rate\ of\ discount)$. Therefore, for the first discount we get: $(300)(100\% - 15\%) = (300)(0.85)$, For the next 15% discount: $(300)(0.85)(0.85)$

11) Choice C is correct

$4 \div \dfrac{1}{3} = 12$

12) Choice A is correct

The width of the rectangle is twice its length. Let x be the length. Then, $width = 2x$

Perimeter of the rectangle is $2\ (width + length) = 2(2x + x) = 72 \Rightarrow 6x = 72 \Rightarrow x = 12$

Length of the rectangle is 12 meters.

13) Choice A is correct

$$2x + 10 = 48 \rightarrow 2x = 48 - 10 = 38 \rightarrow x = \frac{38}{2} = 19$$

14) Choice A is correct

$$average \ (mean) = \frac{sum \ of \ terms}{number \ of \ terms} \Rightarrow 86 = \frac{sum \ of \ terms}{50} \Rightarrow sum = 86 \times 50 = 4300$$

The difference of 94 and 69 is 25. Therefore, 25 should be subtracted from the sum.

$$4300 - 25 = 4275, mean = \frac{sum \ of \ terms}{number \ of \ terms} \Rightarrow mean = \frac{4275}{50} = 85.5$$

15) Choice E is correct

$$average = \frac{sum \ of \ terms}{number \ of \ terms} \Rightarrow (average \ of \ 6 \ numbers) \ 15 = \frac{sum \ of \ numbers}{6} \Rightarrow sum \ of \ 6 \ numbers$$
is $15 \times 6 = 90$

$(average \ of \ 4 \ numbers) \ 10 = \frac{sum \ of \ numbers}{4} \Rightarrow$ sum of 4 numbers is $10 \times 4 = 40$

$sum \ of \ 6 \ numbers - sum \ of \ 4 \ numbers = sum \ of \ 2 \ numbers$

$90 - 40 = 50$ average of 2 numbers $= \frac{50}{2} = 25$

16) Choice C is correct

$x + 5 = 8 \rightarrow x = 8 - 5 = 3, 2y - 1 = 5 \rightarrow 2y = 6 \rightarrow y = 3, xy + 15 = 3 \times 3 + 15 = 24$

17) Choice B is correct

The probability of choosing a Hearts is $\frac{13}{52} = \frac{1}{4}$

18) Choice B is correct

From the choices provided, only $\frac{1}{3}$ is greater than $\frac{1}{5}$.

19) Choice A is correct

2,500 out of 65,000 equals to $\frac{2500}{65000} = \frac{25}{650} = \frac{1}{26}$

20) Choice D is correct

$5x - 6 = 39 \rightarrow 5x = 39 + 6 = 45 \rightarrow x = 9$, then $3x + 6 = 3 \times 9 + 6 = 27 + 6 = 33$

21) Choice A is correct

the population is increased by 10% and 20%. 10% increase changes the population to 110% of original population. For the second increase, multiply the result by 120%.

$(1.10) \times (1.20) = 1.32 = 132\%$, 32 percent of the population is increased after two years.

22) Choice A is correct

First, find the number. Let x be the number. Write the equation and solve for x.

150% of a number is 75, then: $1.5 \times x = 75 \Rightarrow x = 75 \div 1.5 = 50$. 80% of 50 is: $0.8 \times 50 = 40$

23) Choice E is correct

Plug in 104 for F and then solve for C.

$$C = \frac{5}{9}(F - 32) \Rightarrow C = \frac{5}{9}(140 - 32) \Rightarrow C = \frac{5}{9}(108) = 60$$

24) Choice C is correct

The perimeter of the trapezoid is 50.

Therefore, the missing side (height) is $= 50 - 8 - 12 - 6 = 24$

Area of a trapezoid: $A = \frac{1}{2}h(b_1 + b_2) = \frac{1}{2}(24)(6 + 8) = 168$

25) Choice D is correct

If the length of the box is 24, then the width of the box is one third of it, 8, and the height of the box is 4 (half of the width). The volume of the box is:

$Volume\ of\ a\ box = (length) \times (width) \times (height) = (24) \times (8) \times (4) = 768$

"Effortless Math Education" Publications

Effortless Math authors' team strives to prepare and publish the best quality SSAT Mathematics learning resources to make learning Math easier for all. We hope that our publications help you learn Math in an effective way and prepare for the SSAT test.

We all in Effortless Math wish you good luck and successful studies!

Effortless Math Authors

Visit www.EffortlessMath.com
for Online Math Practice

www.EffortlessMath.com

... So Much More Online!

- ✓ FREE Math lessons

- ✓ More Math learning books!

- ✓ Mathematics Worksheets

- ✓ Online Math Tutors

Need a PDF version of this book?

Visit www.EffortlessMath.com

SSAT Middle Level Math Prep 2020-2021

Made in United States
Orlando, FL
06 July 2023

34813311R00083